Contents

CADOGAN

Cadogan Guides
West End House
11 Hills Place
London W1R 1AH

The Globe Pequot Press
6 Business Park Road
PO Box 833
Old Saybrook
Connecticut 06475–0833

Copyright © Helen Truszkowski 2000

Editorial Director: Vicki Ingle
Series Editor: Matthew Tanner
Editing: Matthew Tanner
Series Administrator: Becky Kendall
Proofreading: Kate Paice
Indexing: Karin Woodruff
Production: Book Production Services
Book and cover design by Animage
In-house Designer: Kicca Tommasi
Photography by Horacio Monteverde

ISBN 1–86011–991–3
A catalogue record for this book
is available from the British Library
Printed and bound in Italy by Printer Trento srl.

Acknowledgements

Reprinted by permission of Fourth Estate Ltd,
The Shipping News by E. Annie Proulx.
Copyright © 1993 by E. Annie Proulx.
© Elizabeth Luard 1996. Extracted from *Family
Life* by Elizabeth Luard, published by Bantam
Press, a division of Transworld Publishers. All
rights reserved.
© Sue Townsend. Extracted from *The Secret
Diary of Adrian Mole aged 13³/₄* by Sue
Townsend, published by Random House Group.
All rights reserved.
Reprinted by permission of John Murray
(Publishers) Ltd, *On a Shoestring to Coorg* by
Dervla Murphy. Copyright © Dervla Murphy.
© Gerald Durrell. Extracted from *My Family and
Other Animals* by Gerald Durrell, published by
Penguin. All rights reserved.
© Esther Freud. Extracted from *Hideous Kinky*
by Esther Freud, published by Penguin. All rights
reserved.

Cadogan would like to thank

NOMAD TRAVELLERS STORE
& MEDICAL CENTRE

for the generous loan of their products
for photographic purposes.

About the author

It was during a holiday in Portugal at the age of 19, and a 2-month backpacking tour of Europe a year later, that Helen Truszkowski developed an unquenchable thirst for travel. Helen went on to train as a school teacher in Brighton, but in 1989 the lure of bright lights (and big tour operators) brought her to London, where her travel experiences and innovative writing style won her rapid acclaim as a travel copywriter and photographer. Over the past decade her journeys have taken her around the globe including six months working in South Africa; she has contributed to a range of magazines worldwide, and worked with many of the leading travel industry names. She is a former travel editor of *Executive Woman* magazine.

Her son George took his first flight to New York in 1995 aged six weeks, and toured South Africa at just five months. His mother's constant travel companion, George is proving to be a formidable research assistant. Helen now divides her time between London and Southern Spain.

Contributors

Dr Ivan Stoyanov MD has practised Paediatrics for ten years. He is a Clinical Fellow in Paediatrics at the Queen Elizabeth Hospital for Children, now part of the Royal London Hospital, Whitechapel and proprietor of the Villa Nursery School, in southeast London.

Janet Mills is a highly experienced primary school teacher who has worked in London since 1989. She lives in London and has three children.

Acknowledgements

My appreciation goes to Rachel Fielding and Vicki Ingle for trusting in the seeds of this book, and especially to Vicki and Mat for helping me shape it with their sound editorial advice. Jenny Young has helped tirelessly with the research. Ivan Stoyanov found time in his hectic schedule to supply professional medical expertise. Thanks go to Tim de Bono and Julian Simon for their valuable contributions, and to some of my youngest friends for their unique input. Special mention must be made to Rohan for his loyalty and to Rose, Piotr, David, Andrew, Peter and the rest of my family, who continue to be so overwhelmingly considerate and supportive.

To the memory of my grandmothers,
Agnieszka Naruszewicz, and Bud,
for whom I have so much respect.

Preface

Travel is my business. It has played an integral part in my life; and never more so than the moment I conceived this book. I sat nervously on a bed in a cramped hotel room in Cape Town, while a sickly 5-month-old George fiddled impatiently with his toes and threw me an unimpressed enquiring glance. The truth was, I was stumped. My sense of utter loneliness and inadequacy sent me rushing to the airport to take the next flight back to London, and home to the security of what I knew best.

This watershed convinced me that preparation, solid advice and practical information were what travelling parents needed most. Yet few pointers seemed to exist. Certainly there were none to hand when I was most in need of support.

In the light of this, my confidence grew steadily. Passport in hand, I set out to compile a book of common-sense advice specifically aimed at guiding parents and carers around the pitfalls of travel.

The laughter and tears that George and I have shared on countless trips since, the mistakes, discoveries and hazards we have encountered, and the friends we have made along the way, have all helped to forge this book into something which will, I hope, reassure parents who also want to take their kids far away from home.

Take it from me: venture abroad with children, and you find that you not only survive, but actually enjoy yourself. This book is designed to make the whole experience that little bit easier.

Introduction

Children change everything.

Demanding, frustrating, captivating, unfathomable and loveable as they are, nothing is ever the same once they arrive, including the way we travel. So much changes in fact, that many parents give up the idea of going abroad altogether and settle for the easy option – anything else can seem too daunting, too difficult, or simply too expensive.

Take the kids travelling sets out to help parents and carers confronting the issue of travelling with children, whether it is their first time or not. It is designed to help you choose a holiday, organize transport, and get support along the way. Whether your kid's a picky eater, you are on a budget or a lone parent, or your family is plagued by motion sickness, this guide provides all the advice you need.

Take the kids travelling highlights the best parts, and at the same time warns of some of the more negative aspects of taking your children abroad. While it may seem offputting at times, this is a book which sets out to tell the truth. Forget pages filled with inflated tales of intrepid travel; here, a few real-life anecdotes tell it like it is.

A range of ideas for combating boredom are at hand to help you cope with fidgety youngsters. The medical section by paediatrician Dr Ivan Stoyanov offers sound advice on established medical treatment, as well as a range of

easily administered com-
plementary remedies.
Cautionary health and
safety tips are included,
not to dissuade
parents from travelling
with their children –
quite the reverse – but to offer
reassurance.

The essential message of this book is
that parents need only a few time-
saving techniques, some down-to-
earth advice and a handful of cost-
cutting strategies to make taking kids
abroad child's play (well, almost).
For a child, travel is always exciting,
however daunting the prospect for the
adults in charge. Remember, though,
that the time will come when they
refuse to go on a family holiday at all –
so make the most of it while you can.

choosing a family holiday

Everyone was suitably impressed/censorious/envious/incredulous when I announced that soon I was going to Mexico to live with a millionaire in a jungle. But then a friend came to stay, who had just returned from India, and as we talked a most delightful feeling took possession of me.

Dervla Murphy – *On a Shoestring to Coorg*

When you are finding out about a holiday, it is a good idea to become a cross between Sherlock Holmes and Philip Marlowe. Investigate every angle, be tenacious and firm in your questioning, find out everything you can from the mass of available travel sources. Do not expect to solve the riddle of where to go and what to do overnight. Far better to make an informed choice, and to make it in your own good time.

In recent years, the tourism industry has made a real effort to focus on services for families and their children and to keep up with the changing demographics of its customers. Many tour operators and travel services are now geared up for the family market and do all they can to cater for every interest and preference.

The difficulty is, with so much to choose from, finding the right holiday to suit you requires groundwork, plus free time to do the groundwork – a precious commodity for the parents of young children. So, just where do you start?

Planning the right destination, accommodation and activities can be a daunting task at any time. Make a snap decision and you could end up not only disappointed, but out of pocket too. When children are involved it is even more crucial to be as well organized as possible before taking off. Get it wrong and both you and they will suffer.

Getting started

The most important thing to remember is that time, money and your family's own special needs influence what you will manage and what you will enjoy. Think about places you might feel happy and relaxed in. Then consider whether there will be any scope for your children. It's worth taking some time to make an honest evaluation of your family's strengths and weaknesses, dreams and realities.

▲ Work out a practical holiday budget so that you know exactly how much you can spend.

▲ Your children's ages will have a clear impact on the choice you make. Choose a holiday to suit each of your children's age groups to ensure no one feels left out.

▲ Carefully consider your family's stress levels and plan a holiday that will work around them.

Bear all these factors in mind when you are doing your groundwork and be realistic about your expectations. A month in a remote Buddhist monastery may be your idea of heaven but will your boy-crazy teenage daughter be quite so keen?

Budgeting

Once you have assessed your outgoings, you will need to decide how much you can afford to spend comfortably. There may be other things in your life you are willing to give up to pay for the holiday you feel you need. If not, then you could consider spending just a few days away this year until you have had time to save for something more grand. Maybe an expensive trip need not be part of your plans at all. As far as most children are concerned, a weekend camping trip close to home can be just as much fun as an extended tour of a foreign country. At the end of the day, you will want to be sure that the money you spend and the enjoyment you get are worth the compromises you may need to make. It all comes down to priorities.

What age?

Babies

Babies are surprisingly adaptable travel companions. They are mostly happy to go wherever you go, and love looking at new and interesting things (even if they do not know the difference between Manchester and the Maldives). You rarely have to go out of your way to keep a baby occupied. Comfortable in pushchairs or baby carriers, they are easily transported and they will fall asleep just about anywhere. The biggest drawback to travelling with infants is the array of equipment and accessories they inevitably need, so holidays with an established base are usually best.

Toddlers

Toddlers are undoubtedly the most difficult age group to travel with. Notoriously difficult to keep restrained, prone to mystifying temper tantrums and capable of becoming lost in a flash, they can be exhausting to both themselves and their parents. The good news is that children of this age are invariably enthusiastic, and insatiably curious. They take delight in the smallest things but you will need both incredible patience and a holiday packed full of quick-fire, child-friendly diversions.

School age

This is the easiest age. Children still have the eagerness and interest of their younger years but are more independent and far less labour intensive. They can appreciate cultural visits and have the physical and mental ability to undertake somewhat more challenging excursions. On the downside, they are quick to develop very specific likes and dislikes and unless you are prepared to take these into account early on, you will be heading for big trouble.

Lets go surfing!

You can begin surfing before you even reach the beach on the World Wide Web. Where else can you find instant and accurate updates on destinations, operators, tourism offices, resorts, availability and prices right at your fingertips?

CheapFlights
www.cheapflights.co.uk

City.Net
www.city.net

Hotel Net
www.u-net.com/hotelnet/

Internet Travel Services
www.itsnet.co.uk

Lonely Planet
www.lonelyplanet.com.au

PCTravel
www.pctravel.com

Travel With Kids
www.travelwithkids

Virtual Tourist
www.buffalo.edu/world/

Yahoo Travel
www.com/Recreation/Travel

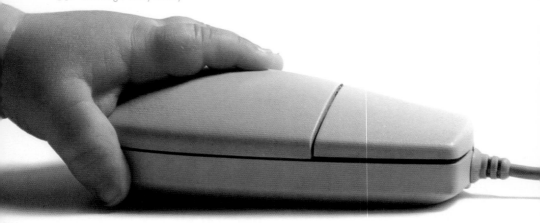

Teenagers

Teenagers can be a nightmare. Trapped between their childlike dependency and a burgeoning drive for adult independence, and with powerful new hormones coursing through their veins, they present a challenge. The primary focus for any teenager is spending time with other teenagers, so it is best if companions are a guaranteed part of the trip. If you want to limit opposition, you will need to negotiate a holiday with a high degree of activity, variety, freedom and the chance to meet others of the same age.

Stress levels

You know your family better than anyone, so you are sure to know the things that make them irritable and uncomfortable. There are aspects of just about every holiday that can make people feel tense, ill and moody. Some of us are terrified of flying; others suffer motion sickness; many more cannot endure intense heat or cold. Some don't like to go away at all. So long as you identify these stress points far enough in advance, you should be able to devise a plan that works around the various potential difficulties.

So much can hinge on a successful holiday, it is little wonder that making decisions can give you palpitations. What adults often forget, when they are agonizing over where to go, or how much it is going to cost, or whether everyone will enjoy it, is that for children the experience of travelling is almost always going to be exciting. So be sure to involve the kids right from the start. Encourage them to pore over the brochures with you, scan the Internet or take a trip to the bookshop. That way, the older ones will have a stake in the success of the trip and the younger ones will have a good idea of what to expect. And, who knows, they might come up with a brilliant idea that has passed you by.

Finding out more

Travel agents

The peace of mind you can gain from having an experienced travel agent working on your behalf may be worth the inevitable added costs. Once the agent knows your tastes, all you need do is offer up a basic idea of what you want and let him or her take it from there. The trick is to make the most of their first-hand knowledge and resources. Simply wading through piles of glossy brochures with an agent is not only time-consuming, but bewildering. What they usually fail to disclose is their range of under-the-shelf travel trade books. These industry 'bibles' cut through the waffle and give you the facts. Ask for the low-down on a destination using their *Gazetteer* or *Official Hotel Resort Guide*. If you have specific ideas about where you want to stay, what you want to do, or how you plan to get there, suggest they delve into one of their OAG Guides instead of flicking laboriously through glossy brochures. OAG publish an in-depth air atlas, world airways guide, cruise, ferry and rail guide, holiday guide, worldwide hotel guide and international travel guide. Any discerning travel agent will have an up-to-date copy of each of these and ought to make full use of them.

Unfortunately, agents who really know the family market are a rarity. Most have a vested interest in booking you on specific airlines or into large chain hotels and resorts. Huge incentives from the holiday and tour operators tempt many to maximize their commissions and bonuses, while cutting down on the time they spend with you. The flurried pace of some travel agents is deliberate. More than offering an efficient service, they aim to book as many customers as they can in as short a time as possible. What is more, their preference for a favoured supplier may not always get you the best deal.

A good agent will be dedicated to finding the best destination and facilities to suit you, at the right price. Be pushy, if need be, and don't allow them to bully and bounce you into making a decision. Travel agents' livelihoods depend on serving their customers' needs.

contacts

English Tourist Board
✆ UK (020) 8846 9000

further reading

Disability Now
✆ UK (020) 7383 4575
A monthly newspaper which has holiday ideas and regular reviews on holidays in the UK and abroad written by people with disabilities.

Family Travel
✆ UK (020) 7272 7441
Quarterly newsletter providing factual and practical travel information, supported by reader's own experiences.

Family Travel Times
✆ US (212) 477 5524
www.familytraveltimes.com
Published bi-monthly. Offers up to the minute news on family travel.

Time Out Kids
✆ UK (020) 7813 6018
Monthly magazine offering a full up-date of events for families in and around London.

The Green Travel Sourcebook by Daniel Grotta and Sally Wiener Grotta, John Wiley & Sons.
The Traveller's Handbook edited by Miranda Haines, Wexas Publications.
Which? Holiday Destination, commissioned and researched by the Consumers' Association.

AITO

The Association of Independent Tour Operators represents many of the UK's smaller specialist tour operators. AITO members share a dedication to high standards of quality and personal service. Strict membership criteria, plus a rigorous Code of Business Practice, ensure holidaymakers are protected whenever they book with AITO members. Their excellent *Holiday Directory* provides holiday ideas plus an extensive A–Z listing of AITO operators, including a description of each member's programme along with their contact details. It is available free on ℂ UK (020) 8607 9080 or by ✉ UK (020) 8744 3187.

Tourist offices

National tourist offices exist solely to promote tourism to their country. Contact them and explain the aims of your trip. You should receive a huge bundle of brochures, timetables and maps, even lists of accommodation rentals, free attractions and local children's clubs, in return. Tourist offices maintain hotel lists, often including every licensed hotel in the area, divided into price categories. As a result, the savings you can make (in comparison to using an agency) are not to be sniffed at.

The Internet

Get on-line and make a search under the name of a place you are interested in. You will be amazed at the sources that pop up on screen. There is no limit to what you can find, and details are often updated daily. Print out any information you need and you will soon have your own personalized guidebook. Since websites come and go with alarming speed it is difficult to recommend specific resources, and the best tactic is often to look via one of the major search engines such as Yahoo, though some sites appear to have become an established base for travellers. *See page 9*.

Travel magazines and newsletters

Newspaper and magazine travel sections, especially at the weekends, are another good source. Destination reports will give you a clear indication of what to expect at holiday spots around the world. Look out, too, for special travel inserts in national newspapers filled with advertisements for individual properties, agencies and special travel deals.

Remember, though, that destination reports won't always be unbiased. Many come off the back of a free press trip, which may weigh opinion in favour of a specific hotel, airline or attraction which has provided hospitality. Few travel magazines and newsletters are specifically written with families in mind, but some that are include *Family Travel* (UK), *Family Travel Times* (US) and *Time Out Kids* (UK).

Teletext

Seek out your own bargain package, airfare or accommodation by scanning the small ads on the Teletext travel pages. Even though the outstanding fares these 'bucket shops' advertise rarely match up to the actual price you are quoted, most do offer substantial savings, especially on last-minute departures. The majority of companies are established and respectable; a few are not. Check for the IATA and ATOL symbols, which will guarantee that your money is safe, even if the company folds unexpectedly. *See page 67* for more tips on reduced-price airfares.

Off-road membership

Breakdown membership often brings its members more than just access to its recovery service. Information centres can provide up-to-the-minute road and traffic information, guidance on travelling overseas, plus maps and details of recommended accommodation. Perhaps most useful of all is the route planning service which can provide detailed routes, tailor-made to suit your needs.

The AA, AAA and RAC produce a range of maps, atlases, leisure, restaurant and camping guidebooks. You can find these in most major bookshops. There are also PC-based software products available which allow you to calculate and print out a range of approved routes and to access inspected restaurants and hotels. On-line systems can offer subscribers information on a wealth of travel-related topics.

Special needs

Families with special needs have a number of additional resources at their disposal when trying to track down the ideal holiday.

BREAK
✆ UK (01263) 823170
A registered charity that provides holiday and respite care for children and adults with disabilities or learning difficulties.

Council for Disabled Children
✆ UK (020) 7843 6000
Information on travel and health.

Guide to travel terms

■ The **Association of British Travel Agents** (ABTA) is a self-regulatory body representing over 2,400 travel agents and some 600 tour operators. ABTA maintains rigid codes of conduct, bonding and accounts rules both for the benefit of its members and to protect the travelling public.

■ An **Air Travel Organizer's Licence** (ATOL) protects you from losing money or being stranded abroad if your travel firm goes out of business. Firms selling air travel in the UK are required by law to hold ATOLs. Travel agents often act for a number of ATOL holders. You should always confirm which one your booking is with and which will appear on your ATOL receipt.

■ The **Civil Aviation Authority** (CAA) is a regulatory body with many responsibilities, including guaranteeing refunds and rearranging travel for holidaymakers who book with ATOL holders that then go bust.

■ The **International Air Transport Association** (IATA) exists to promote safe, regular and economical air transport. Wherever you book, always check for the IATA symbol.

■ The **Association of Independent Tour Operators** (AITO) aims to promote awareness of smaller specialist tour operators and represents the interests of both members and holidaymakers.

■ The **British Airports Authority** (BAA) owns and operates seven of Britain's international airports.

■ The **American Society of Travel Agents** (ASTA) aims to enhance the professionalism of travel agents by identifying and serving the needs of the travelling public.

The Holiday Care Service
✆ UK (01293) 774535
Will provide an information sheet for families with a child or parent who has a particular disability. Their computerized database can provide information about all aspects of accessible holidays and travel in the UK.

Mencap's Holiday Service
✆ UK (0161) 888 1200
Offers a holiday service of respite care breaks and holidays for children with a learning disability.

The Royal Association for Disability and Rehabilitation
✆ UK (020) 7250 3222
Produce three travel guidebooks and three excellent information packs.

Society for the Advancement of Travel for the Handicapped
✆ US (718) 858 5483

Tripscope
✆ UK (0345) 585 641
A nationwide travel and transport information and advice service for the disabled.

A word about hearsay
In light of today's hectic lifestyles, the path of least resistance can often be to follow the advice of friends or colleagues. When you listen to someone rave about a destination, you might be tempted to follow their example before giving it serious consideration. The chances are it will work out just fine. On the other hand, it may not. Of course other people's comments and recommendations are useful, but bear in mind that what works for one parent and child may not work for others.

The classic options

For every family, travelling overseas has different motivations. Ultimately, though, your holiday plans need to revolve around what you most enjoy doing with your children, coupled with what your children most enjoy doing with you – and on their own. The ideal trip should offer plenty of variety and lots of choice for everyone.

One thing is absolutely guaranteed: if your children's holiday is bad, yours will be even worse. But it does not take much of a compromise to choose a holiday that all of you can enjoy. How much you tackle, and where, will depend entirely on your ability to cope with it all. For some, sipping long, cool drinks while the kids dawdle in the mild surf of a beach resort may be enough. Others will hanker after the sights and smells of a city, or the danger of a jungle trek.

The degree to which you favour one option before another will depend on just how desperate you are for a chance to unwind, relax or escape. But don't overstretch yourself, or your children. You know what works for you, and for them. All you have to do is find it.

This section uncovers a range of recognized holiday themes, beginning with the classic options. In addition, there are hundreds of weird and wonderful trips available. To come up with the family holiday that suits you best, you need only use your imagination.

City breaks

The major cities of the world have an irresistible name-brand draw. Paris, Rio, New York, Sydney, Cairo, Beijing – all clamour for attention. Bustling, exciting, overwhelming, with a wealth of facilities right on your doorstep, the great advantage of a city is that you don't have to go far to find something interesting to do.

Children's theatres, museums, playgrounds, parks, shops, theme restaurants and other child-orientated environments are guaranteed. They need to be, because in any city a sizeable segment of the population is its children.

For a first lesson in international awareness, cities are hard to beat. You may be astounded at the memories your children take home, and quite unprepared for the insights they will gain into the culture and

contacts

The London Parents' Guide
✆ UK (020) 7793 1990

Where To Take The Children
✆ UK (0839) 123404
Hotline listing events for children visiting London. Updated daily.

further reading

Doing Children's Museums: A Guide to 265 Hands-on Museums (US) by Joanne Cleaver, Williamson Publishing.
City travel guidebook series. 8+
The Great City Search by Rosie Heywood, Usborne. 4+
Kidding Around, John Muir Publications.

people they met. Children are always fascinated by obvious differences from life at home; the way people dress, eat and play, as well as their local customs. As parents you may casually pass things by. Yet these are the very things that will prove irresistible to your children: the puppet shows and mime artists holding out for a few coins; sitting in a shabby café; examining a building site; wading in a fountain; gaping at the local skateboarders or chasing the pigeons. City streets are a novelty in themselves.

Cities provide the best living museum of history, and unparalleled opportunities to understand the big picture of the past: Roman ruins, Renaissance palaces, baroque churches, dynasty temples. You should not underestimate your children's ability to be captivated by city sightseeing. Statues and towers are interesting anywhere (and make especially good climbing frames, though beware of offending). The starkest architecture can become fascinating once you know a story about it. Even classic literature (and the odd Disney blockbuster) can play its part here. *Peter Pan*, *The Hunchback of Notre Dame*, *Babar* and *101 Dalmatians* all feature capital cities as their backdrop.

Nowadays, junior museums and galleries with push-button exhibits and interactive displays help draw children into the worlds of art and culture with ease. Special city-based discovery centres are often set up especially for children. London Zoo, Philadelphia Please Touch Museum, San Francisco's Yerba Buena Gardens, Brussel's Musée des Enfants and Cape Town's Aquarium are all Meccas for inquisitive young techies.

Things to bear in mind

Stimulating though they may be, cities are often equally crowded and expensive, with an adults-only image that demands more than the usual quota of 'just sit down and behave'. Unless they are used to the lifestyle, the play hard ethic of cities may start to cramp your children's style.

Holidays in a capital city often make you attempt to pack in as much as possible, and sightseeing can feel about as arduous as clambering up a mountain. The trick is not to schedule your time too tightly. You will need to remember to balance active and passive pursuits. You might combine a museum morning with an afternoon picnic; a visit to the local flea market with a game of football in the park. Allowing plenty of time for ice cream breaks should help counterbalance the hectic pace of city life.

In cities, be prepared to use public transport most of the time. Cars can be an immense hassle in any city, more so a foreign one. The last thing you want to do on holiday is bog yourself down with traffic jams, unfamiliar street signs and unclear parking regulations.

Rural retreats

If city life seems all too much then perhaps a spell in the country is the answer. As a refuge from the pressures and routines of modern life, the advantages of staying out of town are obvious. There is plenty of space and fresh air, and unlimited possibilities to explore the countryside, to fish, to hike forest trails or simply to sit and bask in the tranquillity of a secluded setting. In a welcome respite from the clamour of fast-paced cities, here children can immerse themselves in nature and learn about the environment hands-on. From extravagant châteaux and tucked-away cottages to far-flung hill tribe lodges and kangaroo farms, there are country retreats worldwide to suit every budget and taste.

You can count yourself lucky if you find a holiday retreat blissfully devoid of high-rise hotels, nightclubs and marauding hordes, where development has yet to mar its natural surroundings. The sanctuary of a National Park lodge is still a safe bet. Many independent tour operators, too, feature secluded country homes across the globe, ranging anywhere from Icelandic summer houses to a converted Maharajah's palace.

Though you can rent an entire property to yourself, there are also plenty of opportunities to stay within working farmhouse settings, getting to know the local way of life and sharing some 'off the land' home cooking. It is worth checking with national Tourist Offices for their lists of recommended rural properties. In Europe, Austria, Denmark and France are countries in which farm tourism is especially well established.

Rural theme holidays can provide just as much variety. If you children love horses or are enthralled by the Wild West, ranch holidays and bush camps are two popular options. As well as horsemanship, many ranches offer special children's programmes featuring hayrides and wildlife tracking, overnight camp-outs and craft projects. Children are permitted out on the trail from around eight years of age. Some places provide infant care. Each individual ranch has a unique atmosphere. You can choose between rustic accommodation serving hearty, basic fare, or elegant, well-appointed cabins that provide gourmet meals and fine wines.

Travellers who get a taste for pioneer life can progress to more adventurous expeditions, like covered wagon trains, bush trails and cattle drives.

Things to bear in mind

The lure of a rural retreat is the chance to savour a natural and simple side of life. Many people are attracted to the idea of fincas, pousadas, log cabins, watermills – accommodation in traditional buildings renovated with the help of government grants. Gîtes, usually found in the rural parts of France, for example, have to meet standards specified by the government. Despite

contacts

Ferien auf dem Bauernhof
✆ Switzerland (57) 481709
Swiss farmhouses.

Guides des Gîtes de'Enfants
✆ France (1) 4970 7575

further reading

1001 Things to Spot on the Farm by G. Doherty, Usborne. 3+
Farm, Ranch and Country Vacations, Adventure Guides.
The Good Holiday Cottage Guide, Swallow Press.
National Parks: The Family Guide (US) by Dave Robertson and June Francis, On Site! Publications.
Ranch Vacations by Eugene Kilgore, John Muir Publications.

these measures, you cannot expect luxury. Romantic as they sound, these often offer little more than basic levels of comfort. Steep stairs, stone walls, flagged floors, straw roofs and low beams may prove completely unsuitable for your children, especially during damp weather.

It is also worth remembering that farms – like anywhere with large animals and serious machinery – are not the safest places. Your holiday in the country is likely to coincide with the normal working day for the people that live there. You will need to be certain your children understand the importance of following rules, especially around farm animals and equipment.

Beach resorts

From luxurious Caribbean resorts to budget bucket and spade holidays in the Mediterranean, beaches appeal to carefree travellers seeking a classic fly and flop holiday, especially during the grim winter months back home. For parents in need of rest and relaxation, a major draw is that children naturally love to play in water. Whether you rent a beach house or stay at an all-inclusive resort, what your children are likely to remember most are days spent playing at the water's edge. As long as there is water – preferably with a gently shelving sandy beach, rock pools and shells – children will entertain themselves for hours. Beaches provide the ideal opportunity for both you and the children to make friends at leisure with travellers from around the world. Plus there is the chance to practice new skills, such as sailing, windsurfing, jet skiing, snorkelling, surfing, swimming

and diving. Special holiday packages at resorts worldwide are designed to teach a range of water-based skills.

If you are planning a beach destination, of course, you are much more likely to find a holiday that caters specifically for families: the sort of place where you are not punished for bringing the children. Today's family resorts are the modern equivalent of the 1950s holiday camp, though nowadays they are set in far more exotic locations. They are gradually developing to meet demand, but most are still concentrated at the pricier end of the market. The main advantage for parents is their safe purpose-designed, child-centred environment with its wealth of facilities.

contacts

Le Beach Club
✆ US (303) 442 0984
Members' organization that produces a newsletter and members' polls rating of all-inclusive resorts worldwide.

Seaside Awards and Blue Flag Office
✆ UK (01603) 766076
Can provide leaflets on approved beaches in both the UK and Europe which comply with guideline standards.

further reading

Best Beach Vacations: The Mid Atlantic by Donald D. Groff, Frommer.
Caribbean with Kids by Paris Permenter and John Bigley, Open Road.
Florida With Kids, Prima.
Great Undersea Search, Usborne. 4+
Seashore Sticker Book, Usborne. 6+

Babysitting, children's mealtimes, equipment hire and lots of entertainment usually come as standard. One major selling factor is the children's miniclub where weary parents can offload their offspring for daily supervised activities ranging from circus skills to nature hikes or even boat trips to pyjama parties. It is an ideal chance for you all to do the things you enjoy without getting under each other's feet.

If you and your children want laid-back time together (as well as time apart in the company of others of your own ages) this could be just what you are looking for.

Things to bear in mind

For hot temperatures year-round in Europe you will have to go to the Canary Islands or

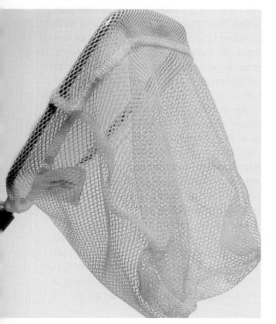

Madeira. If you plan to take the children further afield you may need inoculations.

To go to the Gambia, the Ivory Coast, Kenya and Israel, for example, you are recommended to have vaccinations against cholera, typhoid and polio and to take anti-malarial tablets (for all except Israel). Since you can happily go to places such as Florida, Spain, Greece, South Africa and the Caribbean without having any jabs at all, this may well influence your choice of beach destination.

Wherever you go, check how far from the beach your accommodation is, and whether there are any steps or busy roads to negotiate. In a holiday brochure, unless you can actually see the hotel and the beach in the same photograph, you can bet there will be some sort of distance to travel. Compare the same resort and beach in more than one brochure.

If you stay at a family resort, be prepared for the antithesis of an authentic local experience. You may feel you are giving up all contact with reality in exchange for high chairs by the truck-load but a gratifying, if temporary, respite from the syndrome of 'I'm *boorrred*' may just be worth the sacrifice. Extreme temperatures require you to take sensible precautions. ***See pages 150–1*** for advice on safety in the sun, especially with young children.

Touring

Touring by car, caravan or motorhome allows you to please yourself at a relatively low cost. Free from stuffy schedules, you can take your pick of stop-off points along the way and allow your family both to play and to eat whatever and whenever they choose. When you tour, the day ends as soon as everyone gets tired and you decide to pull off the road. While many hotels, motels, pensions and campgrounds do not require a reservation, you may find you do not make it to one at all. Stopping off at motorway rest areas is both legal and safe in many countries, making it cheap and easy to go as you please. Planning a break at one place for a few days can set an even more relaxing travel pace and allow you time to explore.

Touring suits families of all ages, though it is particularly easy when you have infants who can nap and be fed easily on the move. Older children handle the monotony of long drives better once they are able to entertain themselves, and especially if they are kitted out with the standard personal stereo and a handheld system such as a Game Boy. *See Are we there yet?* for more ideas on keeping them entertained.

Many operators and a few car rental companies rent campers and motorhomes. If you are planning an extended tour it is worth considering the protection in any weather (let alone the added privacy and comfort) that a motorhome or caravan provides. Very young children unfamiliar with sleeping bags, latrines and tents can feel more at ease in a motorhome. Infants, meanwhile, can have all the facilities to refrigerate and warm their feeds close to hand.

You will need to take the time to make lots of enquiries before you settle on a hire deal. Prices vary widely depending on facilities. Motorhomes normally come fitted out with bedding and cooking equipment but ask what else is on offer. A tent, sleeping bags, towels, lights, cooking utensils, crockery, plus folding chairs and tables are useful extras. Expect to pay more for the convenience of a motorhome equipped with a toilet and shower, and remember that you will need to account for the cost of fuel on top. Most motorhomes use diesel and around eight miles per gallon is typical.

contacts

Camping and Caravan Club
✆ UK (024) 7669 4995
http://www.rvrent.com

Caravan Club
✆ UK (01342) 326944

Motor Caravanner's Club
✆ UK (020) 8893 3883

National Caravan Council
✆ UK (01252) 318251

Recreation Vehicle Industry Association
PO Box 2999, Reston, VA 22090, USA
National trade association that publishes a rental directory and helpful booklet.

Roving Women
✆ US (888) 557 8464

further reading

Across America with the Boys by Matthew Collins, MATC Publishing.
Exploring Europe by RV by Dennis and Tina Jaffe, Globe Pequot Press.
Trailer Life Campground/RV Park and Service Directory: US, Canada and Mexico, published annually by Trailer Life.

Things to bear in mind

When your home is on wheels, space is inevitably tight, you won't be able to plan overly-long trips without a break, and there is only so much travelling both you and your children will be able to tolerate. Being cooped up in a vehicle for hours on end is sure to leave you stir-crazy and them bored and agitated and, as with any budget travel, the constant togetherness will eventually cause friction. Be prepared to accomplish long or uninteresting hauls through the night when the children are asleep. Do not count on camping every night either. A night off in a hotel will help ease travel tensions and provide a welcome change.

Before you rent any vehicle you will need to make sure you know how everything works and that everything is in working order. Be sure to find out how much fuel is needed and what maintenance is required. Some campgrounds limit vehicle length to 30ft (9m), so big is not always best. The comedy potential of being stranded with a flat tyre is severely limited so breakdown recovery is a must.

You will also need to invest in maps and guides that describe hotels, motels and campground amenities along with their opening and closing dates and fees. Try to get a good idea of your routes before you leave. Otherwise you will spend most of your travel time fretting about directions and whether or not you should have taken that last exit.

Cruises

A cruise aboard a luxury liner has become one of the best value holiday options for families, regardless of children's ages. More than any other transport, cruise ships allow children the freedom to move around at will once they are underway. What is more, on a ship your home goes with you and, once you are unpacked, sleeping areas, play places, mealtimes and schedules can all remain intact.

Voyages offer plenty for families to do, both on ship and on land. Many cruise ships have facilities and babysitters for the very young; practically all have activities for

further reading

Complete Idiot's Travel Guide to Cruise Vacations by Fran Wenograd Golden, Alpha Books.
Cruising with Children by Gwenda Cornell, Dobbs Ferry.
European Cruises by Harry Basch and Shirley Slater, Fielding.
Great Cruising Vacations by Dorothy Jordan, World Leisure Publishing.
Unofficial Guide to Cruises by Kay Showker, Macmillan Travel.

children of every age. Heated pools, mini-golf courses, supervised clubs, children's menus, interactive game centres and cinemas are all part of the draw for youngsters. Shore excursions offer everybody the chance to dip into the history, shopping, dining and other special attractions of each new port.

Another plus is that an increasing number of the larger cruise liners have many facilities specifically designed for disabled passengers. Celebrity Cruises, Norwegian Cruise Line, P&O Cruises, Princess Cruises and Royal Caribbean Cruise Line can give further information on the services they provide. *See pages 53–4* for contact details.

Package fares make this a surprisingly affordable option when you consider that just about everything is included in the price. Some operators offer children's programmes only on specific cruises – during the school summer holidays for example. These often provide special fares and streamlined activities.

For a more intimate experience, you can also consider a hotel boat cruise. Restored wooden barges and narrowboats are typical of the traditional vessels lovingly converted into luxurious floating retreats. Providing gourmet meals and tailor-made trips to local events and vineyards, these cruises are evocative of a bygone age when service surpassed speed.

Things to bear in mind

Larger and more modern ships come on line so fast that it is hard for travellers to keep up. Bigger ships can mean lengthier walks to get from one place to another. You will need to study deck plans carefully when selecting your cabin.

Be aware, too, that the new mega-liners feature fewer port-stops and more days at sea. Even if they do stop regularly, you could end up disappointed if you were hoping to get a real feel for the ports you visit. Check cruise itineraries to see how long you will be staying in each port and find out

if shipboard programmes focus on the culture of each stop-off point. Programmes on ships in Alaska and Hawaii invariably do, as do most cruises to Central America and the Galapagos Islands.

Secure activity programmes are reassuring for parents with younger children and first-time cruisers, but are sometimes so structured they allow little flexibility. You will need to check whether the clubs are varied enough to suit your children's age groups.

Theme parks

Visiting a theme park has become almost a rite of passage for many families. Most parents will have at least thought about a trip to Disneyland to say 'hello' to Mickey and the rest of his affable pals.

You need make no pretence that you are going just for the children. The reality is that everyone is catered for and just about everyone enjoys them. Most are well maintained and well managed and a whole host of fantasy theme park ideas have been generated along the lines of Disneyland. Sea worlds, water parks and all manner of amusement parks based on special themes aim both to educate and to entertain, ranging from historic to cartoon settings – there is even a park (Hersheypark, in the US) dedicated entirely to chocolate.

At theme parks children are the ultimate consumer and the market meets their desires brilliantly. Few can top the theme park childcare professionals for entertainment value and sheer enthusiasm. Rental buggies, babysitting services, children's menus, theme parades and shows are all part of the fun.

One of the best things about taking a toddler is that under-3s or -4s will almost certainly get in free. They may not be able to go on all the adventure rides, but there is usually a toddler zone with soft play areas and mini rides for them to enjoy.

Things to bear in mind

You can be sure that if you are heading for a theme park there will be ample support services nearby. At the same time a high concentration of tourists inevitably means crowds, queues and high prices. Try to go off-peak if you can to minimize frustration and fatigue.

Theme parks can also be *too* exciting and you will need to be realistic about just how much a young child will appreciate, enjoy, or remember. Children under the age of five will have a good time so long as you do not plan to see everything. Any child over five is sure to remember and relive the adventure into adulthood.

further reading

Amusement Park Guide: Over 250 Amusement Parks (US) by Tim O'Brien, Globe Pequot Press.
Birbaum's Walt Disney World for Kids, for kids and by kids, Hyperion.
Brit's Guide to Orlando, Florida and Walt Disney World by Simon Veness, Foulsham.
Euro Disney: The Mainstream Unofficial Guide by Tania Alexander, Mainstream Publishing.
Unofficial Guide to Disneyland by Bob Sehlinger, Simon and Schuster.

Activity and adventure holidays

One of the hottest areas in travel these days is adventure. For many, sitting on a tour bus or taking day trips from a hotel seems too dull to contemplate. Outdoor activity and adventure holidays appeal to an increasing number of holidaymakers and more accessible and less expensive modes of travel – along with increasing international cooperation – have opened up the globe to visitors. The possibilities seem endless: river rafting, abseiling, wilderness hikes, jungle boating, rock climbing, ballooning, helicopter safaris, cattle drives, dogsledding – these provide just a taste of what is on offer. Make no mistake, adventure holidays are not for those who don't like to get their feet wet, and present an element of risk that other holidays do not. These sort of trips inevitably test your abilities and endurance. At the same time they promote independence, a willingness to try something new and a sense of achievement, so important for children.

Camping

All children love to camp. They enjoy the freedom of the outdoors and the laid-back atmosphere, the chance to explore natural surroundings, to discover wildlife and to meet new lifestyle challenges head on. It can certainly be a welcome relief from PlayStation and Cartoon Network. Moreover, starting to camp early in life (from two years onwards) prepares children for all types of travel. They soon adapt to entertaining themselves more fully, and begin to appreciate the natural wonders each new environment has to offer. In short, it is a good way to toughen them up.

Many countries permit free camping provided you are not too near anyone's home. However idyllic the setting, of course, pitching your tent on open ground means you won't be able to rely on even the most basic of facilities. You will be completely on your own. There may be no one around to help you pitch your tent in the pouring rain, no washing or toilet facilities and no provisions nearby. These problems may seem

further reading

Adventuring with Children by Nan Jeffrey, Avalon House Publishing.
Complete Buyer's Guide to the Best Fodor's Family Adventures by Christine Loomis, Fodor.
Great Adventures with Your Kids by Dorothy Jordan, World Leisure.
Outdoor and Recreation Equipment by Nan Jeffrey, Avalon House Publishing.

trivial from the comfort of your home, but it is wise to imagine the worst before setting off into the wilderness with your billycans and pak-a-mak.

Organized campsites, on the other hand, have toilet and shower blocks, shops and entertainment, making them ideal for families. What they may lack in privacy and even aesthetics, they certainly make up for in social interaction. Nowhere is it easier to meet people. It is a real bonus, of course, when there are plenty of other children to play with.

More civilized still are sites where luxury tents come ready-pitched and fully equipped for use. No khaki army-surplus tents here. Most family tents are large, apartment style tents, divided into separate rooms by zipped partitions. They feature transparent window panels and tent sides which can be raised to extend living space whenever weather permits. Most have all the mod cons; some even have their own separate toilet tent. It is often worth the additional expense of having your own bathroom facilities as traipsing through wet grass with children in the early hours is never much fun. Sites such as this usually give a great deal of thought to families, often providing organized children's activities, babysitting, baby-equipment rental, plus strict noise and speed restrictions.

Things to bear in mind

When comparing what companies have to offer, the cheapest deal may not represent the best bargain. It is essential to compare site facilities before you book.

These vary considerably, from the most basic to the sublime. The range of campsite amenities needs to be a major factor in helping you to make up your mind. While a self-catering holiday will certainly save you money, do consider whether you will really want to cook every day. The takeaway food outlets, supermarkets and restaurants on some sites can prove a major advantage, especially as a social focal point. Check too how far the site is from the nearest town or beach; whether there is a regular bus service, laundry facilities, equipment to hire, a swimming pool or something to pass the time if it rains.

The more popular the location and well-equipped the campground, the more crowded it will be. Sunny, coastal locations are the most crowded and often attract seasonal campers who use permanently booked sites as their second home.

contacts

British Tourist Authority
✆ UK (020) 8846 9000
Can provide a list of camping and caravan parks in the UK.

Caravan Club
✆ UK (01342) 326944
Can provide a handbook on continental sites.

further reading
Camping and Caravanning Sites, published by Michelin annually.
Camping Out by Heather Amery and Stephen Cartwright, Usborne. 3+
Traveler's Guide to European Camping by Mike and Terri Church, Rolling Homes Press.

Cycling

Despite the fact that nearly all children love to cycle, parents seem slow to realize the potential to channel this enthusiasm into a family trip.

Cycling provides a passport to freedom and a wonderful way to introduce young children to adventure. While the pace remains steady and the scenery constantly changing, you certainly experience more on a bicycle than you ever could speeding past in a car. Moreover, it is an experience the whole family can share. Children who are too young to ride alone can watch, fascinated from the vantage point of their child seat or trailer. Older children (from around seven years) can relish the independence of covering the open road under their own power. Any child big enough to ride a 10-speed bike can go touring and carry full bicycle gear.

There are a number of organized bike tours and camps that include guided rides, beginner routes, instruction, bicycle and equipment rental and accommodation. The advantage of a planned tour is that everything is taken care of. The tours are graded by difficulty, so if you are in doubt of your ability, you can always choose something

easy to begin with. Once you are on your way, you can enjoy all the benefits of exploring natural surroundings by day and retreat to the comfort of your hotel at night. There may even be options for short routes and van pick-up support in case you get tired early. Despite the convenience of it all, the tour operators that offer organized hotel-based cycling holidays rarely recommend taking children still in nappies.

If you have sufficient time and equipment you can plan a do-it-yourself bike trip and allow for the difficulties that bringing along an infant entails. For low-cost and low-key travel, you need only map out your routes and places to stay, pack the essentials, prepare some snacks and pedal off into the great yonder. First timers with toddlers might prefer a series of day trips from a central base, more ambitious families with older children may consider an extended country tour. Indeed, if you plan to tour a country where bicycles are the primary

contacts

Headwater Cycling
℡ UK (01606) 813333
Escorted or independent cycle tours to France and Italy. Can take blind and partially sighted holidaymakers with a sighted companion.

mode of transport, cycling can be an excellent way to help alleviate the disparity between lifestyles (it can certainly allow for a mutual respect seldom seen between tourists and locals).

Many areas have designated bicycle paths, others only have terrain that lends itself best to mountain biking. In countries where large distances need to be covered between areas of interest, most public transport will accommodate bicycles for a small fee.

Things to bear in mind

The destination and terrain need to be chosen carefully. For first timers it is best to head for a warmer and drier climate since clothes can be kept to a minimum and camping is a more viable prospect.

Do not plan your tour as though you are training for the Tour de France. Keep the pace relaxed and allow plenty of time for rest stops.

The volume and weight of equipment are limiting factors so remember that you will only be able to carry the essentials. Bicycle dealers often overwhelm you with an arsenal of gear, clothing and accessories, none of which you need. Unless you are travelling with a holiday company which offers to transport your suitcases from stop to stop, you will only be able to take enough belongings to fit into a pannier or rucksack.

Very often it is easier to hire or even buy a bicycle locally. Unless you are planning an organized bike tour, however, child seats, helmets and panniers, including front bags and supports, are the few things best bought from a bike specialist at home. In the developing world these are not only less

likely to be available, but any equipment in the shops may be of poor quality. Buying them could risk your entire family's safety. *See pages 96–7* for safety advice on travelling by bicycle.

Trekking

In the last few years trekking has become increasingly popular. Many trekking companies now offer wilderness pack trips with horses, llamas, mules or plain backpack, each off the well-trodden tourist track and each graded for difficulty. Organized trips average from 3–8 miles (5–13km) per day

contacts

Accessible Adventures
℡ US (802) 496 2252
belliott@madriver.com
Tours throughout Vermont designed for travellers with special needs.

Wilderness Inquiry
℡ US (612) 379 3858
A non profit organization which strives to bring all kinds of people – especially those with disabilities – into the American wilderness.

further reading

Sigma Publishing
℡ UK (01625) 531035
Produce a range of books which can help plan walks in the UK with children.

Parent's Guide to Hiking and Camping: A Trailside Guide by Alice Cary, W.W. Norton. *Spotter's Guides* series, Usborne. 8+

for starters. Most are suited to children of all ages; even babies are commonplace.

It is a mistake to believe that these type of holidays only appeal to seasoned walkers. The footpaths of the world are often an integral part of a country, and trekking across them offers more than just an energetic stroll. Trekking can bring you into intimate contact with an area at a pace children will enjoy. Unlimited opportunities to stop, linger and explore are all more attune to children's needs and interests than a tour experienced from the confines of a bus or car.

Using an experienced guide has its advantages. Organized tour guides work in the same areas year after year and know their areas in detail so they can offer a level of safety that individual trekkers find hard to match. Alongside this, they can provide all the necessary equipment. There is very little point in kitting yourself out with compasses, topographical maps, fire starters and radios unless you plan to make trekking a long-term family pursuit.

As for four-footed companions, of course, the natural affinity between children and animals help make these organized treks all the more memorable. Caring for and feeding the animals is often part of the trip.

If you are determined to go it alone, in some areas you can hire porters or support vehicles to carry your packs and your children. Often it is not even essential to carry camping equipment, for along many popular routes you are likely to find strategically placed huts, inns and lodges where you can rest up and eat.

Things to bear in mind

From around six years children can carry their own framepack. It is unlikely that they will be able to manage a full-sized daypack until they are around 10. Hence, packing should be kept to the bare minimum. Forget the make-up bag. A Swiss army knife, first-aid kit, torch and matches are the sort of essentials you will need. On this type of holiday a few favourite toys, high-energy snacks and a roll of toilet paper are likely to become your idea of luxury.

It is important to invest in a pair of boots which fit over the ankle. They will need to be durable and waterproof with a non-skid sole. If you want to avoid painful blisters, remember to break them in at home.

You won't be able to push yourself as hard as you may like, or expect too much from your children. You especially won't be able to go too high or too far with youngsters. They do not acclimatize to high altitudes as easily as adults and serious problems can result. Children flag quickly in the afternoon, so the more strenuous trekking is better done early in the day.

Along the way you will also need to take numerous breaks to rest and eat. While lots of stops are essential, that won't mean that you are off the hook. Remember that your children will provide a never-ending source of things to do, whether they need feeding, washing or entertaining. You may need to consider whether such frequent stops will impede the progress of your tour. Unscheduled delays may not be fair on other trekkers, so make sure you know the rest of the team's goals before you set out.

As intoxicating as the landscape is, traipsing through it is unlikely to enthral your children for long, especially if they are toddlers. A youngster's idea of fun is throwing stones and digging with sticks in the dirt. To them, passing it all by may not make any sense. The success of a family trek will ultimately boil down to your sensibility and your child's adaptability. Your children will need plenty of encouragement along the way; be prepared for low points in their morale. One solution might be to organize a tour with other families, as children often enjoy trekking more when there are others of their own age around to motivate them.

Boating adventures

Catamarans, barges, kayaks, canoes, sailboats, dinghies and motor yachts – sailing provides plenty of holiday opportunities for families. Take your pick of self-steer hire and barefoot charters, through to crewed yachts and shore-based sailing options. Whichever you plump for, you will find you children cannot wait to help out with rowing, steering or mooring. Moreover,

contacts

The Association of Pleasure Craft Operators
✆ UK (01952) 813572

British Tourist Authority
✆ UK (020) 8846 9000
Can provide a list of waterways in Britain and Ireland.

British Waterways
✆ UK (01923) 226422

Royal Yachting Association
✆ UK (023) 8062 7400
Also run an independent charity, RYA Sailability, that promotes and coordinates sailing for disabled people.

United States Sailing Association
✆ US (401) 849 5200 www.ussailing.org

Waterway Houseboat Vacations
✆ Canada (250) 836 2505
Operates a wheelchair-friendly boat equipped for passengers with special needs.

further reading
Cutaway Boats, Usborne. 10+

the easy accessibility of activities such as swimming, fishing and snorkelling provides plenty of added adventure.

Whether you want to fine-tune your skills or start with the basics, approved sailing classes are available from tour operators, charter services, marinas and many local community projects worldwide. It is down to you whether you take a course before you leave home or wait until you arrive; either way, proficiency can be acquired fairly rapidly. In fact, even a novice can learn to sail a small boat in a matter of hours.

Several organized packages are purely instructional and can offer you the opportunity to learn how to sail a wide variety of craft. These are not generally suited to children under nine years however, and some companies have even more rigorous age limits. Other tour companies specifically cater for family needs and can even provide junior courses for children as young as five, where they will learn to sail dinghies. Crèche and babysitting facilities are provided by many of these operators.

Once you are an experienced sailor, of course, there is nothing to stop you chartering a boat and taking it where you please. Making a decision on the right type of boat will depend on cost, the amenities on board, your special interests and the make-up of your family group. You will also have to decide whether you want to hire someone to get (and keep) your boat afloat.

Both tour operators and independent charter firms can arrange transport and ferries to help you reach your destination. All will provide information on the waters you are exploring and on how to manage the boat. It is common for fuel to be included in the cost, and even damage waiver insurance.

If you would rather do more sightseeing than steering, then you may decide to hire your own seasoned skipper. Charter boats (both skippered and independent) will often accept children of all ages, providing safety harnesses for toddlers and buoyancy aids for all children other than babies.

For families, flotilla sailing is a safe bet. This allows you the freedom to skipper your own yacht. At the same time it offers you the security of travelling in a small convoy following the lead boat, with a trained captain and crew to navigate and help out en route if necessary. For this sort of holiday at least one adult on your boat must have some sailing experience or have taken a short flotilla sailing course prior to the holiday. A second adult is necessary on each boat to help with mooring.

Away from the high seas, self-catering waterway holidays are always popular, especially on the peaceful canals, rivers and lakes of Europe and the USA. The pace is slow, the focus in-depth and the exposure to nature intimate. In general no experience is necessary, as waters are consistently calm, often shallow and speeds average just 3mph (5kph).

Canoe trips, too, provide another ideal way to explore protected areas worldwide at a serene pace. Canoes offer the independence of boat travel without the expertise and cost of sailboats. Although space is limited, a canoe can easily accommodate two adults and two children.

River rafting provides for perfect family adventure, as again experience and special skills are not required. Family raft trips are

increasing in number, and come complete with guides chosen as much for their ability to work with children as their rafting skills. Families with younger children generally stick to float trips in moderate white water, Class I to II rapids. For added thrills, families with teenagers can opt for rivers with more intense white water.

Keep an eye out for family camps around the world. Many of these will be set in spectacular mountain or lake settings. These learning centres feature programmes that often include elementary sailing, canoeing or kayaking.

Things to bear in mind

When selecting a boat check the bathroom facilities, and whether heating and linen are provided. Galleys should be fitted with cooker, fridge, crockery, cutlery and cookware. You will also need to make sure you are well stocked since provisions are not so easy to get once you are afloat. Most boats now also include TVs. All should come equipped with deck equipment, including lifebelts and a mooring rope or anchor.

One of the obvious difficulties on boats is the confined space, which can be a problem with toddlers and energetic youngsters. Not every boat is right for every child and, without exception, all operators recommend that you hire a larger boat than you actually need.

Beyond the risk of falling in the water, sailboats can present fewer risks than the average home. Yet safety is critical. Remember that everyone will need an approved life preserver specifically designed for the type of area in which you will be sailing. Children are advised to wear these at all times. Small children can wear a fitted life jacket or a buoy float which fits around their chest, but you may also need to consider harnesses for children under the age of three, plus safety nets to allow them enough scope to move above and below deck. If you cannot hire or borrow safety equipment, try mail-order marine catalogues.

Once you set sail you will need to familiarize yourself quickly with the area you are sailing and be prepared to listen to the weather forecast carefully to avoid storms or heavy rains. With children on deck you will need to be vigilant at all times. Bear in mind that rough seas will necessitate keeping your children below, which is bound to lead to frayed tempers all round, not to mention sea sickness.

Skiing

Skiing's up-market image still exists in resorts such as Aspen and Gstaad. At the same time a growing demand for winter holidays that do not cost a fortune has spawned many companies and new resorts. In fact, fierce competition among tour operators has brought benefit to all skiers. Nowhere is this reflected more than in the discounts offered to families. Children aged 2–12 years are eligible for a range of discounts, dependent on their sharing a room with two full-price adults. These discounts can be offered as a flat fee, a price reduction or a percentage discount. It really does pay to compare; many companies use the same accommodation, yet charge vastly different amounts.

A large number of family package operators offer classes for children of all ages and also provide their own nursery and childcare facilities for the youngest family members, supervised by qualified staff. Out of hours babysitting can usually be arranged through the company representative or local tourist office. If you book independently, you will need to rely on childcare services offered by the resort nurseries. The main drawback here is that there is likely to be little guarantee of either staff competence or English language skills. A medical certificate of good health is sometimes required as a condition of entry to a resort-run crèche.

Most ski resorts offer half-day and full-day skiing programmes for children aged between 3 and 12 years, which usually include instruction, lift pass, rental equipment, food and supervision.

Besides skiing, of course, winter resorts offer an eclectic mix of adventure sports including snowboarding, skating, sledding, sleigh riding, snowmobiles, even wolf tracking. For easygoing family skiers, cross-country trails can provide a more adventurous and less costly alternative to downhill. Avoiding the noisy, crowded lift lines, you glide across empty, silent fields. There is less chance of injury, and children who do not take readily to the slopes may enjoy learning to cross-country ski instead. Both groomed and ungroomed trail systems cater for skiers of differing abilities. Besides ski lodges, there are customized multi-day tours or even single-day ski classes which provide opportunities for cross-country ski adventure worldwide.

Things to bear in mind

There seems to be a difference of opinion about the appropriate age to take babies to ski resorts. Some operators advise against taking very young babies; others welcome them, from new-borns onward. Remember that extremes of cold, even brief exposure, can threaten a baby's health while bright sun reflected off the snow can damage delicate eyes.

The best skiers do not necessarily make good ski guides. Certified instructors not only know how to ski, they have also studied how to teach. First judge whether your child will be happy left alone with relative strangers. Check, too, whether your instructor has trained to work with children. Many package operators will provide English-language ski lessons, convinced that this helps children learn more happily.

Bear in mind that children learning to ski will need plenty of encouragement and praise for whatever progress they make. First timers can find skiing a frustrating experience. Be sure to find a resort which offers easy access to the slopes for all skiing abilities. Children find walking in ski boots difficult, and you won't enjoy carrying their skis and poles on top of your own.

When picking a resort, travelling time, particularly transfer time to the resort itself, is important. This may range from one hour to close to three – difficult with small children, especially when there are no child seats on transfer coaches.

The expense of a ski holiday is not just down to travel and accommodation. The most important aspect of planning a family ski trip is ensuring that you are all properly prepared. For beginners, renting ski equipment at the resort is often best. Children grow out of equipment quickly and will need to upgrade their skis as their skill levels improve.

Clothes are a different matter. Given that in general you get what you pay for, these are rarely cheap. Borrowing can save significantly, or you could consider a second-hand source. Either way, properly insulated bib overalls and a jacket, roll-neck pullovers, water-resistant socks, ski mittens and a hat are best for children (you run the risk of scarves becoming caught in lift machinery). The emphasis needs to be on quality outerwear. Novice skiers fall over a good deal of the time. Being cold and wet won't help their progress, and risking hypothermia will put the entire trip in jeopardy. Helmets are a useful safety measure, as is plenty of sunblock and a pair of high quality ski-goggles or sunglasses. Winter sunlight reflecting off the snow at high altitudes can be especially intense.

contacts

Erna Low – Adaptive Ski
✆ UK (020) 7548 2841
ernalow@easynet.co.uk
www.ernalow.co.uk
Family ski holidays providing independent skiing for people with a physical disability.

Virgin Ski Trains
✆ UK (01273) 748482

further reading
The Best Family Ski Vacations in North America by Laura Sutherland, St Martin's Press.
The *Good Skiing and Snowboarding Guide* edited by Peter Hardy and Felice Eyston, Which? Books.
Where to Ski and Snowboard edited by Chris Gill and Dave Watts, Thomas Cook.

Wildlife encounters

A growing realization of the tremendous importance of the environment, especially among the young, has opened up the entire area of eco-travel. The largest growth area is tours which help shape our relationship with creatures great and small.

Forget the long-range binoculars. Nowadays you can choose between a holiday on which you literally come face to face with a wild animal, or one on which you keep just a little more distance between you, supported by a guide as you observe them at incredibly close range.

Though there are many holiday opportunities, the nature of these expeditions usually appeals to independent travellers aged between 18 and 45. Many tour operators do their utmost to discourage children. Those that do welcome youngsters do so by paying a lot of attention to detail. Safaris and expeditions designed for families normally feature carefully selected lodges and reserves, and they move quickly, without dragged-out waits and lots of strict timetables. If you are determined enough, there is always the opportunity to take a self-drive tour with your own vehicle and even camp, though with children you are best restricted to tarmacked routes and fenced-off campsites such as in South Africa's Kruger Park.

From iguanas in the Galapagos to humpback whales in Byron Bay; from gorillas in Uganda to lions on the Serengeti, the benefits of teaching children about animals and giving them a chance to get up close are clear enough. A nature trip to where the wild things are provides immediate and

A ranger speaks

Julian Simon is an experienced ranger who has worked extensively in South Africa and Uganda. He has this to add:

'Some of the more remote and up-market lodges will not allow any children below a certain age (normally around 12). It can be an awkward situation taking children on safari as their wants and needs do vary greatly from those of adults. Their concentration span is shorter, they can't sit still in one place for too long, they need meals at different times and they talk at different noise levels. All these factors have to be considered to allow everyone to enjoy the experience to the fullest, both parent and child.

If a child has no interest at all, or is younger than four years, then it is not advisable to take them along. Most lodges that allow children have minders, nannies or a babysitting service. A few offer special activities specially targeting children, such as Bush School or holiday programmes.

My suggestion is to book a safari where your family are the only clients assigned to a ranger for the duration of the stay, so all activities can be tailor-made to suit you. This has very little impact on anybody else and makes it all the less stressful for the parents. Though it is generally more expensive (as other seats that could have been filled have to be paid for) the added flexibility makes it money well spent.'

long-lasting rewards. What is more, wildlife encounters actually benefit the animals too. Tourist money provides a good deal of research funding.

Things to bear in mind

There is still much debate about the age at which children will get the most out of this type of encounter. Travel may be in anything from converted lorries to helicopters and air-conditioned coaches, but is usually always on uneven trails which can prove exhausting even for a healthy, active adult. It is worth remembering that though children are resilient and adaptable, the majority of tours are in out-of-the-way locations and a doctor is rarely included on the team. Children may need immunizations before they leave home to protect them from any number of life-threatening diseases, including malaria and yellow fever. You will need to take along basic medication too (such as cough syrup, antihistamine and even antibiotics) which can be hard to find in the developing world. *See Medical matters* for further medical advice.

In areas where the weather and conditions are extreme you will need to take advice about proper clothing and emergency procedures. Only you can decide what is best for your child, so carefully weigh up of the pros and cons before making a commitment to this type of holiday.

Several operators express concern that children's crying or chattering can disturb the animals that everyone has travelled so far to see. A baby's cry, in particular, is said to be at the same frequency as that of as a wounded animal. Attracting lions eager for a kill will not enhance your holiday experience. Hence, children under eight years are often excluded from private game reserves and children under five are rarely permitted on game drives, especially in open-sided vehicles. Game drives tend to last at least three hours, and it is usually up to the ranger to make a judgement about whether any child has the patience or interest to sit through it. Your safety is paramount to the rangers and they will need to weigh up the situation accordingly.

There is also the further concern that, in their eagerness to live up to the promises of their brochures, safari operators openly encourage their drivers to get as close as possible to the wildlife. This is not always desirable. It is important to try and sift out the tour companies that are more interested in adventure than in the protection of animals. By choosing a trip carefully, you help ensure future generations will be able to share in the magic of these intimate encounters too.

Archaeological digs

Digging in the dirt comes naturally to children. What is more, history tends to stick when children can actually see and touch something that belongs to the past. It makes a much stronger impression than books alone. Uncovering archaeological ruins and artefacts not only offers you a chance to learn about the ways people once worked, lived and played, but also a good deal more about yourself.

Just as extraordinary are the palaeontology research sites where you can dig for prehistoric bones and fossils. Dinosaurs may be extinct in the real world, but on these sites they seem about as alive as your children would like them to be.

In recent years scientific research sites all over the world have started to provide holidaymakers with a unique and rewarding opportunity to contribute to their work efforts. Most expeditions are run by non-profit organizations and you are invited on site very much on a volunteer basis.

With so many valuable and fragile materials to hand, parents and children are taught the proper way to dig and to handle finds, and you do not need special skills or knowledge to take part. Discussions about the project, lectures and hands-on instruction in excavation are all part of the experience. Some programmes also include hikes and day trips. You might even get the chance to assist in a real laboratory.

One added benefit of these research projects is that they provide the ideal opportunity to meet people from different cultures and backgrounds. Off the well-beaten tourist track, it is a chance really to get to know a new place, especially when local residents provide the housing.

Though some sites are quite undeveloped, others are in towns with modern conveniences and amenities. Accommodation can range from community tents to hotel rooms. Knowing what conditions to expect can help you find the tour that best suits your family.

Things to bear in mind
Dreams of a big find are part of the draw to this type of holiday. You should not have unreasonable expectations however. Check how many finds have been unearthed at your site in advance.

Archaeology and palaeontology can be painstaking, slow, dirty and tedious. Sites are generally hot and dusty and often require hours of digging in uneven and rocky terrain. Consider whether your child has sufficient interest and the right personality to enjoy this type of trip. It is demanding work. Before you book, discuss your child's ability, experience and interest with somebody who has been on-site

Volunteers are often separated, working at different activities or in different areas of the site. Sometimes lodgings also separate the sexes. This might mean a single parent sleeping apart from their child. If this is unlikely to suit you, be sure to check well ahead of time.

contacts

Council for British Archaeology
✆ UK (01904) 671417
100271.456@compuserve.com

Dino Times
✆ US (516) 277 7855
Monthly children's magazine which includes news on current dinosaur studies.

further reading
Dino-Trekking: The Ultimate Dinosaur Lover's Travel Guide by Kelly Milner Halls, John Wiley & Sons.
Fossil Factory: A Kid's Guide to Digging up Dinosaurs, Exploring Evolution and Finding Fossils by N., D. and G. Eldredge, Addison Wesley Longman.
The Great Dinosaur Atlas, Dorling Kindersley. 7+
Where Did Dinosaurs Go? by M. Unwin, Usborne. 6+
Where Dinosaurs Still Rule by Debbie Tewell with Gayle C. Shirley, Falcon Press.

going it alone or buying a package?

For some, really getting under the skin of the place they visit matters most. If that is you, a few years ago you were probably happy backpacking through India. Yet it is a sad fact that, once children arrive on the scene, a lot of once intrepid parents become reluctant to venture far from home. It is usually nothing to do with losing the spirit of adventure. Without the voice of experience to offer advice and reassurance, it seems many of us become too hesitant to take a risk.

Having decided what you want from your holiday, the next step is to decide who is best equipped to supply it. You will already know whether you are the type of holidaymaker who likes to have every detail planned for you in advance, or whether you prefer to arrive and see how things turn out. You could even find yourself resorting to a little of both.

Even if you relish the thought of choosing a destination, phoning for brochures and quotes, and making all the reservations yourself, you may still need the help of travel professionals. Nowadays package tours are geared to a variety of tastes and expectations. Even if you like to steer well clear of 'designer' holiday culture, using an operator can still make sense. It is feasible to book just your accommodation or holiday programme through an operator and arrange transport to your destination yourself. A package operator can provide just transport too. Though this is unlikely to be your cheapest option, it may be just what you need if you find you are becoming bogged down with the whole time-consuming booking process.

Going it alone

No parent wants to appear reckless. Nonetheless, the thought of postponing a solo trip until the children are older will unsettle any parent who has developed a passion for independent travel and adventure. If travel means limiting your family to tame and easy holiday options, it probably won't seem worth the effort. But if making your own way is what you are used to, then children need not hinder your sense of wanderlust. If you want to go it alone, you can.

Independent travel means holidaying outside the secure itineraries and supervision of tour representatives and guides. It is much easier to feel exposed and vulnerable when you are travelling alone, especially in areas still relatively untouched by tourism. Taking children along brings with it an added sense of responsibility, and rightly so. Your pace and outlook on the world certainly change once you travel with children. That single-life approach of reckless adventure is at once replaced by a good deal of caution and planning, and packing and patience suddenly become critical. How you travel, where you stay and what you eat all need to be considered more carefully. Children are often more prone to sickness than adults and standards of medical care can be extremely variable worldwide. Make no mistake. It takes guts to venture off on your own.

Yet, despite the hassles, going it alone with your children is a rewarding experience. Pursued on your family's own terms, independent travel can offer the chance to develop all sorts of skills, not least social. Children have a wonderful way of opening doors and breaking down cultural barriers. However different your language, customs or lifestyle, parents share a universal empathy. Naturally undaunted, inquisitive and, for the most part, uninhibited, your children will lead you into the sort of encounters with other parents and children that you might never have envisaged.

Away from familiar surroundings and home comforts, independent travel means facing situations far from the established norm. You will find yourself having to cope with situations you may not fully understand, let alone feel in control of. Yet the sense of accomplishment will far outweigh the temporary setbacks. In today's world, where success is often equated with the accumulation of all things material, this kind of challenge can present your family with a whole new set of criteria for achievement.

How child-friendly can a self-drive tour of Australia or a four-week trek through the jungles of Belize be? In fact, children are incredibly adaptable. The more remote your destination, the more diverse the people, the more they are likely to take to it. So long as you know you can relax and enjoy the experience, they will follow suit. The rest of your family and friends are likely to be the only ones that need convincing.

Be realistic

Once you have allayed your own anxieties about travelling with your children and fended off the pessimism of family and friends, you will need to get practical. However independent-minded you are, you cannot just up and leave. However much you have enjoyed casual travel in the past, any independent family trip requires proper planning. You won't be able to avoid making the decision of where to go, assessing all your needs and abilities, and doing enough advance groundwork to ensure the trip is a success.

You are certainly more likely to take well to independent travel if, as a family, you are busy and sociable, and your children are acclimatized to strangers. It won't help if your home life is highly structured and has strict routines that cannot be easily adapted as you travel. While basic rituals help children wind down from the excitements of the day, you will need to be open to letting regular bedtimes and mealtimes drift when something else gets in the way.

Faced with a household of possessions it can be hard to know what to take, especially when you are not going to be dependant on tour staff or waiting taxis to help you along the way. Unless you want to become a beast of burden, pack just the essentials. If needs must, extra clothes and toiletries can be bought just about anywhere in the world.

Whenever you go it alone, you are sure to face a few difficulties. Expect delays, cancellations, lost luggage, missed transfers, over-booked flights and restaurants, closed attractions, and worse. When something goes wrong, you will be forced to deal with it yourself. Whatever attitude you adopt, your children are sure to adopt too. Respond to snags with anger and frustration, multiply that by the number in your family, and you will soon see where that leads you. A stressed-out parent inevitably equates to a tearful and even fearful child. If you are committed to travelling your own way, then you will need to be prepared to keep your cool, maintain a sense of humour

Don't panic!

The number one rule for all travellers is to prepare for the worst, and hope for the best, as even the most well worked out plans can go horribly wrong.

▲ Keep an emergency supply of books and games to divert the children while you plan what to do next.

▲ Take extra clothes, nappies and snacks in your hand luggage. Though you have no control over diversions, delays and lost luggage, your children's understanding will dwindle as soon as they need something.

▲ To avoid disappointment always carry a guidebook so that you can find something else to do nearby.

▲ If your travel plans fall apart, think about every possible alternative before you decide to head back home defeated.

▲ If you miss your connection, you may be able to take another flight or train to a stop-off point close by and hire a car to drive to your destination.

▲ Adopt a positive attitude and you may find those around you are more willing to be helpful.

and make the most of setbacks; that way your children will take your cues and begin to learn the importance of patience and flexibility – both critical when there is no one else around to back you up.

Do your homework

It isn't only children who have to do their homework. When it comes to holidays, seeking out the best deals for your transport, accommodation and added extras is sure to be most important. If you plan to do a lot of independent travelling, it is always worth investigating the special passes and discount tickets that are available. It can especially work in your favour if you are travelling outside established dates and durations. The one- or two-week holiday is practically a cultural institution. While some international airlines give bargain rates for trips under three weeks, often the longer you stay, the greater the discount. *See Saving money* for money-saving ideas, especially on reduced airline fares.

 If you have an idea where you want to go geographically, but you are still uncertain about where to stay or even what to do while you are there, then consider subscribing to a local publication from the place you want to visit before you even leave home. Not only will you get a feel for who lives there and for what is going on, but you may also find little-known gems through reading the reviews and features.

 When touring, it is probably not worth trying to book your first night's accommodation ahead of time, unless you are absolutely guaranteed a place or you are heading for a crowded capital city. Unless you are planning to stay in luxury hotels, pre-booking is often unreliable anyway (despite the ease of phones and faxes and the fervent assurances of travel agents). Until you see a place for yourself you cannot really judge whether it is up to standard or even what it

will cost. The last thing you want is to end up somewhere you don't like for more than you wanted to pay. Instead arm yourself with a destination guidebook, get the latest word on the Internet, contact the national tourist board for listings and tear out any newspaper article recommendations. Then take your pick once you arrive.

Friends and family

Personal contacts are helpful whenever you travel. They are even more useful in compulsively sociable countries such as Brazil and Italy where family ties mean everything. Scan your old address book and ask everyone you know for personal connections in the country you are travelling to: your partner's mother in Pennsylvania, a long-lost friend in Melbourne, an old colleague in Kampala, the furniture salesman you once had drinks with in Cape Town. It is always worth getting in touch with them, especially when your only alternative is a characterless apartment surrounded by equally clueless tourists. Ask them to send you some local newspapers so you can get an idea about the place before you arrive. They may even be able to give you leads on cheap accommodation and flights.

Delays and connections

If you are heading somewhere that involves connections, allow as much time as possible to make the change. Then still expect things to happen differently. Unavoidable mishaps – missed flights, wrong turnings, delayed trains, lost luggage – are common enough when travelling, and it is not unusual to be stranded and left wondering what on earth you should do next.

Though unexpected problems are impossible to avoid, so long as you are prepared the whole episode can still become more laughable than catastrophic.

Once you arrive

Unless you have pre-booked, finding a place to stay is likely to be your top priority. If you arrive exhausted, forget about bargain-hunting for the first couple of nights. Find a comfortable, relaxed place to stay with the children and, once you are sure you like the area enough to stay, go looking. Try to familiarize yourself with the area before you make important decisions, especially if you are on a budget. The first few days are sure to be the most expensive anyway. Locals always keep a keen eye out for visitors who are new to a place and do not have a clue about how the system works. So don't worry about the rip-off hamburger and fries that cost a fortune and were virtually inedible – there will be plenty of time for economizing later.

Once you have found some accommodation you like the look of, check all the facilities over and use your discretion to assess whether it seems reasonable for the price you are being asked to pay. If it seems dear, negotiate. Locating all the amenities from scratch can be daunting. To avoid having to find shops that are open, bring along everything you might need for the first day or so, including food. The first 48 hours are a time for recuperation and getting to know a place at leisure, not rushing out to buy bread and toothpaste.

One thing you should try to do early on if you are visiting a country for a long stay (especially if there is a chance of civil unrest or a natural disaster) is to register at your nearest embassy or consulate. This will make it much easier if someone at home needs to contact you urgently, or in the unlikely event that you need to be evacuated in an emergency.

Otherwise, with no set itinerary or travel commitments, allow yourself to improvise. Apart from the time you leave home, the place you head for, and the date you are due back, the trip can become an open opportunity. If you allow the holiday to develop each day at a time, there is no telling what will happen along the way.

Take time to stop at tourist information offices. They are excellent advice sources and can often help you with anything from accommodation to emergency hire equipment. You might learn about a festival, museum or craft show you weren't aware of. Ask, too, about organized guided day tours. These can give you an overview of the area and a better idea of where you may want to spend more time.

Do not expect to grasp the appeal of a new place immediately. The charm of a country is often more subtle than you have been led to believe. Still, if you arrive in a place that turns out to be a mistake, do not be afraid to move on, even at the risk of losing money. It is better to forfeit your local currency than the entire trip. The main attraction of independent travel is being able to make your own decisions and change your plans. Remember, there is nothing locking you into a certain place or situation except your own actions.

Buying a package

Unless you consider yourself a competent traveller and you are used to exploring on your own, then you are probably better off booking a package.

Turning over the logistics and management to a tour operator certainly gives you more time to enjoy yourself. Tour reps and guides who have travelled extensively in an area will know local people and places that are inaccessible to independent visitors. They will have the necessary equipment, training and knowledge to keep your family safe in a new environment and to help you deal with any problems that may arise.

Moreover, organized packages allow families to travel to places they could never manage on their own, whether it is down to lack of expertise, because for some places it is difficult to obtain permits and visas, or simply because booking their trip independently would cost too much.

Best of all, family package tours that include other families will provide your children with an instant supply of playmates of similar ages. Included in the package there is likely to be scheduled backup, with itineraries, organized activities and various kinds of suitable entertainment and meals, all planned with children in mind. You can also expect most of the guides, reps and couriers to have specific childcare training.

All-inclusive

All-inclusive resorts, as pioneered by Club Med, have become a popular family travel option. All meals, entertainment, sports and facilities are set up so all you have to do is enjoy the experience. Having paid one all-inclusive price, there are no surprises, no hidden costs and no bills mounting up for the daily activities and endless snacks that are part of any family holiday. The security of knowing that one price covers everything will allow you to relax, without worrying about any of the details. Since there are no budget restrictions the children will not have to limit their fun and you will be able to

do as much as you please just about whenever you choose.

On the down side, there is always a chance you will get weary of dining in the same restaurant night after night. Look out for imaginative resorts that feature theme nights and varied activities. Bear in mind, too, that all-inclusive hotel rooms can be smaller than most standard hotel rooms. Check before you book.

Tailor-made

If you want to step out of the familiar, but cannot find a ready-made package to suit you, then a tailor-made holiday could be the answer. A personalized travel service specializes in advising, planning and arranging itineraries for individual travellers, whatever their needs. Letting somebody else plan your holiday down to the last detail has its obvious advantages. Years of extensive first-hand experience enables tailor-made operators to provide in-depth knowledge and reductions across the board. They can start from the beginning and create a made-to-measure holiday that is yours and yours alone. Cost aside, the only thing to limit you is your imagination.

Age matters

Many trips and certain activities have age restrictions, especially adventure packages. Other family operators who make a big noise about welcoming children may only provide childcare for new-born babies and toddlers at a select few of their resorts. Do ensure that your chosen destination will provide childcare for each of your children's age groups. Check, too, whether there is flexibility for children to join a friend or sibling in a different group.

Children's clubs

Many resorts, hotels, cruise ships and campsites provide supervised children's clubs. They offer an ideal way for your children to make new friends, often with others their age from around the world. They can help teach your children about a new place or culture in fun ways, and introduce them to sports and activities you may have no time, aptitude or inclination for yourself. Even more importantly, they allow you time to indulge yourself without interruption. Sheer bliss.

On the other hand, not all clubs are created equal. The majority of children's clubs have no official regulations, and they vary widely in terms of quality care.

At the very least, you should expect individual name bands and a medical history sheet to ensure your child's safety. Before your own children attend, try to drop into a session while it is in progress.

Make sure all is well and be wary of staff who spend more time talking to one another than to the children. Keep an eye out for children who seem glued to the TV screen. Are different age groups lumped together? Are scheduled activities regularly cancelled with little notice? Check whether the staff have appropriate training, experience, resuscitation and first-aid skills for the age group they are supervising. Make a note, too, of the ratio of children to adults. In most nurseries and care facilities this is regulated but holiday resorts are not obliged to follow the same practice. The ratio is a major safety issue, especially if children are near the beach or pool. The ideal ratio is no more than three infants, six toddlers, 10 pre-school or 15 school age children per staff member. Do not hesitate to complain if you feel safety or security is being compromised, especially if staff seem unwilling to discuss your concerns.

Deals and discounts

There are many fantastic deals for families on the market and, as the amount of disposable income per family gradually increases, travel companies try harder and harder, each vying to make you part with your hard-earned dough. Your best bet is to keep your eyes open for offers in the newspapers and travel agent windows and take note of weekly media updates offering advice and special bargains.

Many operators advertise free places for children, but be sure to read the small print before you get too excited. In general, if you do not mind sharing a room with your children (usually up to two) you are eligible for a substantial saving. It is often best to contact the company direct and not to rely totally on the advice of travel agents, since the small print in brochures is notoriously confusing. At the same time it may be worth your while checking the size of a room you are expected to share, as the holiday company's idea of how many beds fit in one room may differ considerably from yours. Other questions worth asking include

▲ How far in advance do we need to book our holiday?

▲ How much of a deposit is required, and when is the balance due?

▲ Is there a supervised children's programme at the destination?

▲ Are there any hidden or additional charges, and will I be expected to tip?

▲ What is your cancellation policy?

▲ Is travel insurance included in the cost?

Booking

Bear in mind that it is essential to request everything that you need when reserving your seats. If you book through a travel agent, ask for confirmation of your requirements. Meals, cots, bassinets, special room or seat allocations: travel services, and especially airlines, are often willing to supply anything so long as they are properly requested with enough prior warning. Yet often a tour operator or agent will fail to make your request, or simply will not make it clear enough. Any agent or operator who fails to take notice of your requirements risks being in breach of contract. For peace of mind it is worth checking with your carrier 24 hours before departure to reiterate your needs.

To find out exactly what children's facilities each travel service has to offer, it is always best to contact the tour operators direct. If you are unhappy with any aspect of the service you receive, write asking for compensation proposals as soon as possible. ABTA's code of conduct obliges agents and operators to acknowledge complaints within 14 days, and to send a detailed response within 28 days.

Booking – the classic options

Travel companies are successfully providing novel tours and special family-orientated facilities each year. Listed below are some established names and telephone numbers to help you begin planning. This listing is in no way comprehensive, though all the companies included here either cater particularly for families or provide an interesting or unusual service.

Many companies are new on the market, others are esoteric and some are strictly for the established specialist. These listings should provide a good start for further browsing and help you get a feel for what interests you. Each concise entry does little justice to what these companies have to offer and the details provided are simply intended as a guide to the operators' programmes. Contact them direct and check for current prices and special offers.

Family packages

Airtours
✆ UK (08701) 577775
Flexible children's clubs at around 60 properties for 3–10 year olds. Their Family First programme is dedicated to making holidays easy on parents with under-3s. Airtours also run a family ski programme.

British Airways Holidays
✆ UK (0870) 242 4245
www.british-airways.com
Dedicated programme of upmarket holidays worldwide, including tailor-made tours. Can advise on accommodation that is particularly child-friendly. Their Florida programme has been especially designed for families.

Cosmos
✆ UK (0161) 480 5799
www.cosmos-holidays.co.uk
Affordable Mediterranean holidays with a strong emphasis on families. Free children's meals, babysitting, crèches, stroller hire, Starbugs and Cosmic Cats children's clubs, child discounts plus a teenagers' InZone at selected hotels.

Crystal Holidays
✆ UK (020) 8241 5030
travel@crystalholidays.co.uk
The Pepi Penguin Club at six of its self-catering properties in France is for children aged 6 months plus. They also offer a nanny share scheme and a Flying Nanny Service for families staying in their private French villas. Crystal Holidays also have a family ski programme.

First Choice
✆ UK (0870) 750 0100
Entertainment is geared towards family time together as much as apart, plus separate supervised teenage activities. First Choice feature provisions for children in a range of their Mediterranean brochures, plus a family ski programme.

Kuoni
✆ UK (01306) 742888/000
Wide programme of upmarket global holidays. Child facilities available at various locations worldwide.

Rascals in Paradise
✆ US (415) 978 9800
Just for families, providing a good selection of cultural trips worldwide that are especially accommodating to children.

Scott Dunn
✆ UK (020) 8767 0202
Upmarket European villas with a resident nanny providing childcare eight hours a day on a flexible basis, including babysitting; plus a chef five days a week. Their Ocean and Islands programme recommends specific resorts, individually rated for their child-friendliness. Includes a family ski programme

Sunworld
✆ UK (0990) 550440
Kidsworld programme at around 60 properties, including beach parties, face-painting and early pirates' supper.

Thomson
✆ UK (0990) 143503
Mediterranean superfamily programme at around 21 hotels: childcare six days a week, pre-bookable equipment, children's buffet, safety-standard playgrounds, play centres for different age groups. The more budget-conscious Skytours programme has kids' clubs at 36 Mediterranean properties. Also a family ski programme to Europe.

Virgin
✆ UK (01293) 616261
Have their own children's clubs at Mediterranean venues, operating for 2–3 hours, six days a week. Virgin also provide some children's facilities year-round at selected hotels and resorts in the USA.

Rural retreats

A Touch of France
✆ US (732) 738 47725
senses@France.com
Includes a 10-day tour on which children are fully entertained and spend five days on a working animal farm. Meanwhile parents explore rural Normandy unfettered. Their varied programme caters for children aged between 6 and 12.

All Canada Travel
✆ UK (01420) 541007
Log cabin holidays in the Canadian outback. Park rangers organize activities such as beaver tracking, canoeing and 'wolf howls' at night.

Australian Farmhost Holidays
✆ Australia (2) 6029 8621
www.travelaus.com.au/farmhost
Operate a central booking office for over 160 host farms throughout Australia, ranging from 3- to 5-star bookings. Families with children are well catered for.

Distinctly Different
✆ UK (01225) 866648
Membership group of around 50 unusual UK properties ranging from windmills to a folly. Most accept children.

The Farm Holiday Bureau UK
✆ UK (01203) 696909
An agricultural cooperative of around 1,000 tourist-board inspected farms offering B&B and self-catering accommodation in the UK.

French Country Camping
✆ UK (01565) 626266
Concentrates on quiet, rural sites throughout Europe. Bicycles are provided on every site. Children of all ages welcome. A subsidiary of Eurocamp.

Helpful Holidays
✆ UK (01647) 433593
A range of holiday homes in the UK provided by a company priding itself on its child-friendliness. Large rental properties for family

gatherings include a fort. A number of properties are on working farms.

Meon Villas

✆ UK (01730) 266561

Traditional Spanish fincas. Many particularly highlight their suitability for families.

Nomadic Thoughts

✆ UK (020) 7604 4408

UKNomadic@aol.com

Tailor-made holidays across the globe featuring exclusive hideaways, including castles and châteaux, log cabins, Himalayan tea houses and a Lisu Hill Tribe lodge.

Oregon Trail Wagon Train

✆ US (308) 586 1850

Accepts children aged 5-plus. Starting from a base camp in Nebraska the train follows portions of the original Oregon Trail. Guided by real-life cowboys, five wagons for 40 people is typical.

Rural Retreats

✆ UK (01386) 701177

Beautiful, well-equipped houses and cottages throughout the UK; cots, high chairs and babysitters can all be booked.

Simply Corsica and Simply Ionian

✆ UK (020) 8747 3580

www.simply-travel.com

Various creative programmes, holiday hideaways and an Island Wandering option to the Mediterranean's least explored islands. Also feature a private crèche and children's club on both Corsica and Zakynthos.

Sunvil Discovery

✆ UK (020) 8568 4499

www.sunvil.co.uk

Individually tailored holidays around the world, featuring carefully selected retreats

Beware of brochures

Without doubt, this is a magical kingdom that caters for all. An enchanting world of variety and mystery where exotic sights and sounds assail your senses. With its dreamy tropical scenery, glittering temples and beautiful, easygoing people, Thailand delights every taste.

Hype or not, don't forget, most of the travel material you read is intended as a selling tool. Thailand is promoted as a beach and jungle paradise, but brochures tend to gloss over the steaming heat, polluted cities and in many areas, dire poverty. The Trade Descriptions Act 1968 makes it a criminal offence for a tour operator to publish a brochure which it knows (or indeed, ought to know) contains false or inaccurate information. Both consumer watchdogs and the Advertising Standards Authority keep an eye out for brochures that are dishonest or misleading.

Nevertheless, it is always wise to take a copy of the brochure with you on holiday. First impressions can be a letdown, no matter what the brochures, books and travel agents promise. Glossy words and pictures help conjure up an image that may ultimately fall short of expectations. One glimpse and you may be ready to leave.

Bear in mind that the brochure's description, photographs and maps all form part of a contract between you and the tour operator. If the three-room luxury chalet turns out to be a one-room shack with no roof on it, then you will need to claim compensation. Having a copy of the brochure will be extremely useful as evidence.

from bush camps to farmhouses, National Park lodges to paradores.

The Dude Ranchers Association
✆ US (970) 223 8440
Has a directory of over 100 holiday ranches in western USA and Canada.

Beach and family resorts

Beaches
✆ UK (020) 7581 9895
www.beaches.com
All-inclusive family resorts, each featuring a Kids' Kamp, Ultra Nannies service and teenage SegaCentre. Non-stop entertainment to suit just about every age.

Center Parcs
✆ UK (08705) 200300
Purpose-built villages in the UK, Holland, Belgium and France, set on 400-acre landscaped sites with organized activities, kindergarten, adventure playgrounds, a subtropical swimming complex, child-friendly restaurants, and no cars.

Club Med
✆ UK (01455) 852202
www.clubmed.com
The original all-inclusive resorts, operating worldwide with many child-friendly facilities on their family sites. Mainly French-speaking staff and international guests. Florida is especially recommended for families. At some clubs under-5s stay for free.

Complete Caribbean
✆ UK (01423) 531031
Tailor-made holidays to the Caribbean islands. Family hotels and resorts feature strongly.

Eurovillages
✆ UK (01606) 734400
Purpose-built, self-catering holiday villages in France, Italy and Spain, offering a wide range of sports facilities, plus children's clubs from three months to 18 years.

Mark Warner
✆ UK (020) 7761 7000
www.markwarner.co.uk
European resorts with an emphasis on childcare, offering children's clubs six hours daily and free baby listening every evening. Many of their resorts welcome babies. Also have a family ski programme.

Scott Dunn
✆ UK (020) 8672 1234
Selected beach resorts and hotels throughout the Caribbean and Indian Ocean individually rated for their child-friendliness.

Silk Cut Travel
✆ UK (01730) 265211
www.meontravel.co.uk
Island Retreats programme featuring a collection of exquisite beach locations in the Far East, Indian Ocean and Caribbean. You can even book your own private tropical isle.

Other lesser known specialist tour operators who can be relied upon to guide you through the beach resort minefield include

British Virgin Islands Club
✆ UK (01932) 220477

CV Travel
✆ UK (020) 7581 0851

International Chapters
✆ UK (020) 7722 0722

Nomadic Thoughts
✆ UK (020) 7604 4408

There are a wealth of independent beach resorts, and these can be booked easily through an operator such as Virgin, Kuoni, British Airways, Rascals in Paradise and many of the operators listed above. You may want to contact them direct, to see if they can offer you a better deal than the package operators. Some of the most child-friendly resorts worldwide include

Atlantis
✆ Bahamas (242) 363 3000
A spectacular resort built around the Atlantis fantasy theme, offering the largest man-made marine habitat in the world, grottos, river ride, sports center, casino and Camp Paradise children's programme.

Boscobel Beach Resort
✆ Jamaica (876) 975 7331
Pricewise resort near Ocho Rios offering four children's clubs and an exclusive nanny-hire service available at an hourly rate.

Breakers
✆ US (407) 655 6611
Takes child-friendly recommendations from the resort's Kids Advisory Board. Hence, rooms have been redesigned with families in mind, childcare advisors, children's menus (under-3s eat free) and a Coconut Crew Camp for 3–12 year olds are now all part of the resort's programme.

Cap Juluca
✆ Anguilla (264) 497 6666
www.capjuluca.com
A resort which aims to please parents as much as children. A complimentary children's programme, kid's clubhouse and babysitting combine with adult activities and three miles of secluded beach.

Forte Village Resort
✆ Sardinia (070) 92171
A 55-acre site in Pula, on the coast of Sardinia. It's safe for children to wander, and there is a small zoo, cycle hire for all ages, a children's crèche and activity clubs, buggy hire, toddler's restaurant, nightly entertainment and babysitting.

Franklin D Resort
✆ Jamaica (876) 973 3067
Jamaica's first all-inclusive family resort which consistently gets top rating. Children's mini-club, activity centres, sports tuition and a dedicated nanny for each suite all add to the appeal.

Hayman Island Resort
✆ Australia (7) 940 1234
One of the Whitsunday Islands, Hayman Island's renowned beach resort has a year-round children's programme and crèche, along with the usual watersports, plus a PADI dive centre for parents.

Hyatt Regency Coolum
✆ Australia (075) 446 1234
Claims to offer the most comprehensive childcare facilities of any Australian resort. Qualified staff care for kids from six weeks to 17 years.

Kona Village Resort
✆ US (808) 325 5555
Based in historic Kaupulehu in Hawaii, there is a Na Keiki in Paradise children's programme, while children under five can eat and stay for free.

Kurumba Village
✆ Maldives (604) 442324
Superb resort facilities, including a choice of restaurants, children's pool and a range of leisure activities.

Smuggler's Notch
✆ US (802) 644 8851 & UK (0800) 897159
An adventure packed resort village in Vermont welcoming children from six weeks. Includes day-long children's programmes and professionally staffed childcare centre, plus family entertainment.

Sugar Beach Resort
✆ Mauritius (230) 453 9090
Set on the island's longest beach, there is a fully supervised Sun Kids Club and crèche, junior pool, babysitting, plus superb sporting and recreational facilities.

Windjammer Landing
✆ St Lucia (758) 452 0913
Features a series of informal, low-rise buildings nestled among 55 acres of lush tropical gardens. A supervised Children's Village and kid's club for the over-4s, nanny service, child discounts, babysitting, and kids' menu all add to the welcoming atmosphere.

City breaks

City break specialists are rarely much use when booking with children as few know much about the facilities at the hotels they feature. Tailor-made operators and specialists to your specific city destination are likely to be more helpful.

Cadogan Holidays
✆ UK (01703) 828313
www.cadoganholiday.com
Programme includes unusual breaks in and around the Mediterranean. Flexible holiday durations and generous child discounts feature strongly.

Kirker
✆ UK (020) 7231 3333
cities@kirker.itsnet.co.uk
Attractively priced European city holidays.

Travelscene
✆ UK (01733) 894611
marketing.tscene@dial.pipex.com
Over 100 European destinations offering a choice of transport options. A tailor-made service, free printed guides and child reductions are among the extras.

Touring

All-Ways Pacific Travel
✆ UK (01494) 875757
www.all-ways.co.uk
Tailor-made self-drive options to Australia and New Zealand.

Avis International
✆ UK (0990) 900500 & US (800) 331 1084
Can arrange motorhome rentals in France.

Bon Voyage
✆ UK (0800) 316 0194
www.bon-voyage.co.uk
Two-centre motorhome and mountain ranch holidays to the USA. One week and 500 free miles (800km) in a luxury motorhome is followed by a week on the Absaroka mountain ranch in Gun Barrel Canyon.

CanaDream
✆ US (403) 250 3209
Puts together holidays through its rental division, Canada Campers.

Cruise America
✆ US (602) 262 9611
Nationwide rental organization. Offers fly-drive options, allowing you to collect your vehicle in the area you want to tour.

Frontier Adventures
✆ UK (01243) 545214
Individually-planned tours of Canada offering a range of activities, locations and transport options.

Lakes and Mountains Holidays
✆ UK (01329) 844405
lakes@freenet.uk.com
Tailor-made holidays to lake and mountain regions across Europe and Canada. A number of self-drive options are available.

Moswin Tours
✆ UK (0116) 271 4982
Specialist tour operator offering holidays throughout Germany and its neighbouring countries.

North American Highways
✆ UK (01902) 851138
www.northamericanhighways.co.uk
Personal travel service throughout North America providing bespoke touring holidays in areas of outstanding beauty.

Travelmood
✆ UK (020) 7258 0280
Six-berth campervan rental in Australia.

Cruises

Abercrombie & Kent
✆ UK (020) 7730 9600
Traditional barge cruises, accompanied by tailor-made trips to local sights. Babysitting can be arranged.

American Hawaii Cruises
✆ US (504) 586 0631 & (800) 765 7000
Offers children's programmes seasonally, or whenever there are 12 or more children aboard. Both ships offer a youth centre and full-time recreation coordinators who organize activities for 5–16 year olds.

Carnival Cruise Lines
✆ UK (020) 7729 1929 & US (800) 327 9501
Morning to night activities for children in four different age groups, between 2 and 17 years. Baby-sitting also available. Fun Ships include 114-foot-long (35m) water flume slide. Includes a Disney Vacations cruise option.

Celebrity Cruises
✆ UK (01932) 820230
The Celebrity fleet comprises five 5-star ships operating in the Caribbean and off the southeastern American coast.

Costa Cruises
✆ UK (020) 7323 2200
Child-friendly programmes plus a 'cruise saver', which offers savings for children and single parents.

Crystal Cruises
✆ US (800) 820 6663
www.crystalcruises.com
Family-friendly cruise line, including cruises to Alaska, featuring more than 42 shore excursions.

Cunard Line
✆ UK (01703) 716634
The *QE2* takes babies from six months. Babysitting and a crèche are provided on board.

Disney Cruises
✆ UK (020) 8222 1055 & US (800) 551 8444
Three- or 4-day cruise to the Bahamas boasting age-specific kids' programmes from 9am to midnight, plus all the magical Disney touches and leisure facilities you could possibly hope for.

Holland America Line
✆ UK (020) 7613 3300 & US (800) 426 0327
Club HAL for children in four age groups, between 3 and 17 years, run by professional nannies and teachers. Babysitting available.

Norwegian Cruise Line
✆ UK (0990) 906060 & US (305) 445 0866
Programme offering activities year round for ages 6–17 years aboard all vessels, plus kids of 3–5 years during the summer. Includes parties, children's meals and personal appearances by Universal Studio characters.

P&O Cruises UK
✆ UK (020) 7800 2222
All three ships have facilities for 2–17-year-olds. Under-2s must remain with their parents. Daily children's programme and events available as well as babysitting.

Premier Cruise Line
✆ UK (020) 8385 9008
Imaginatively planned clubs to suit five separate age groups, between 2 and 17 years. Single parent and child reductions apply.

Princess Cruises
✆ UK (020) 7800 2468
Minimum age ranges 6–18 months. Some of the line's vessels feature separate children's and teen centres. Five ships have supervised activities from morning until late night. Babysitting available. Child reductions apply.

Royal Caribbean Cruise Lines
✆ UK (01932) 820230 & US (800) 327 6700
Children's clubs for three age groups, between 3 and 12 years plus separate Teen Centre for ages 13–17 years.

UK Waterway Holidays
✆ UK (01992) 550616
Barge and narrowboat hotel cruises through England, Wales and France, welcoming children from 6 years upwards.

Theme parks

Most major travel agents can provide competitive packages to many of the world's theme parks. It is also worth contacting individual theme parks direct to see if they can offer you a better deal. A few UK operators who provide a specialized service include

Bridge Travel Service
✆ UK (01992) 456651
www.bridge-travel.co.uk
Their Theme Park programme focuses on six European parks and 15 holiday villages, plus the Walt Disney World Resort in Florida. They have a separate Disneyland Paris programme.

Florida Vacations
✆ UK (01727) 841568
Flexible tailor-made itineraries to the Disney area.

Keith Prowse Attraction Tickets
✆ UK (01232) 232425
A variety of theme park tickets throughout Australia, Europe and the USA.

Specialized Tours – Scandinavia
✆ UK (01342) 712785
Personalized tours to Legoland.

Travelscene
✆ UK (020) 8427 8800
Wide range of travel options and accommodation to visit 12 of Europe's finest theme parks. Child discounts apply.

Booking – activity and adventure holidays

Camping

While all holidays listed below are reputable and proven child-friendly, this is in no way a comprehensive list, and not all will be suitable for your family. Adventure holidays in the US are legion and you will find many more than could possibly be listed here.

Canvas
✆ UK (01992) 553535
Four-star sites throughout Europe, all with free children's clubs four hours a day. Evening pyjama parties, teenager's activities, free travel packs and babysitting.

Carisma Holidays
✆ UK (01923) 284235
Feature French beach sites catering exclusively for families. Children's clubs, babysitting and baby packs provided.

Eurocamp
✆ UK (01565) 626262
www.eurocamp.co.uk
Tomy parent-friendly award winner offering immaculate campsites across Europe with Circus Clubs for 4–13-year-olds. Bebe sites are particularly suitable for under-5s.

Haven Europe
✆ UK (0990) 233777
Owns and operates its own parks in France. A Tiger Club entertainment programme is offered for 4–13-year-olds. Babysitting, games box, baby pack and junior tents are also available.

Keycamp Holidays
✆ UK (020) 8395 4000
Well-equipped campsites throughout Europe providing children's couriers, free club activities and children's pack.

Sandpiper
✆ UK (01932) 868658
A small specialist that knows its sites intimately. Offers detailed advice, children's club, babysitting and free junior tents.

Select France
✆ UK (01865) 331350
Family-run operator offering eight 4-star sites in France. Child-friendly facilities include play areas, pools, Squirrel Club four days a week, plus toys and babysitting.

Sunsites
✆ UK (01565) 625555
Sites throughout Europe including a site close to Disneyland Paris. High quality 4-star facilities include children's activities, fun packs, babysitting, and rental equipment.

Cycling

Backcountry
✆ US (406) 586 3556
Combines biking with one or several other activities. Children welcome from age 6-plus, and van support is available for all. Tours operate in the US, New Zealand, Hawaii, Alaska and Canada.

Backroads
✆ US (510) 527 1555
Families with children aged 2-plus can choose between cycling only or multisport holidays throughout the USA and Europe. Itineraries are relatively slow to suit all ages.

Beics Eryri Cycle Tours
✆ UK (01286) 676637
Feature both guided and tailor-made leisure tours of Wales. Babies accepted from one year. Plenty of equipment can be provided.

Bents Tours
✆ UK (01568) 780800
Leisurely routes through Bavaria and Austria for families with children from around one year. Luggage transfer, plus a range of equipment including both lightweight and trailer bikes.

Breton Bikes
✆ UK (01579) 350379
Run by parents with three pre-cyclers of their own. Offer both independent and guided tours to Brittany. Babies accepted and even a nappy carrying service is offered. Good range of equipment available.

Byways Bike Breaks
✆ UK (0151) 722 8050
Flexible countryside routes through Shropshire; several take in attractions to interest children. Luggage transfer and detailed maps provided. child seats and trailers available. All ages accepted.

Compass Holidays
✆ UK (01242) 250642
Accept children of all ages on their 2- and 7-day graded tours of the UK. Luggage transfer, holiday packs and 24-hour back-up service. Variety of rental equipment available.

Country Lanes
✆ UK (01425) 655022
Cycling holidays in the UK and US with support van and a range of options for children of all ages.

Cycling for Softies
✆ UK (0161) 248 8282
Toddlers accepted with their own cycling gear. Equipment provided for children from three years on their flexible tours of rural France. Regional assistants are based at a Home Base Hotel to provide full back-up. Adult equipment provided and some smaller bikes.

Leisure Activity Safaris
✆ UK (01626) 777903
One and 2-week tours of Kenya with vehicle support and luggage transfer. The youngest to attend so far was aged four.

Tracks 'n' Trails
✆ UK (01765) 606686
Routes designed with families in mind. Tours of rural Yorkshire, staying in working farms, a watermill, old staging inn and railway station. New hybrid bikes each season, plus trailers, seats and tandem bikes.

Vermont Bicycle Touring
✆ US (802) 453 4811
Cyclists can choose from trips throughout the world, from weekend getaways to 17-day expeditions. Recommended for children aged 13-plus with some biking experience.

Trekking

Alternative Travel Group
✆ UK (01865) 315679
Tailor-made independent walking holidays through Italy, France and Spain. Walks average 10–13 miles daily, although alternative transport is available. Recommended for children aged 10-plus.

American Wilderness Experience
✆ US (303) 444 2622
Provides both customized family trips and an overview of many of the best US horse pack operators, welcoming children aged 6-plus.

Appalachian Mountain Club
✆ US (603) 466 2727
Sponsors too many hiking, backpacking and camping courses to list here. All ages welcome on a variety of imaginative US family workshops and skills programmes.

Avalon Llama Treks
✆ US (704) 299 7155
Llama treks designed for families with children aged 4-plus. Infants in backpacks are also welcome.

Canadian Mountain Holidays
✆ Canada (403) 762 7100
The company divides groups by ability, and also offers a multi-adventure family holiday with walks especially aimed at children. All ages accepted, though over-8s recommended.

Compass Holidays
✆ UK (01242) 250642
UK-based walking breaks with half-price, seasonal reductions for children. Route packs provided.

Exodus Travels
✆ UK (020) 8675 5550
sales@exodustravels.co.uk
Escorted walking and trekking tours to diverse locations worldwide, including camel, donkey and elephant treks. Older children and teenagers can be assessed on an individual basis to ensure they suit the challenging programmes.

HF Holidays
✆ UK (020) 8905 9558
Walking holidays at various UK locations. There are special child reductions throughout the season.

Sherpa
✆ UK (020) 8569 4101
Door-to-door baggage transport plus an accommodation booking service in a growing number of UK walking areas.

Sierra Club
✆ US (415) 923 5522
Family trips for all ages, including babies, though many specifically target certain age groups. Includes treks to glaciated terrain, to Lassen Volcanic National Park, and even a Toddler Tromp.

Southwest Trekking
✆ US (520) 296 9661
Highly customized treks through Arizona and Mexico. The company will put together a trek to suit each member of your family, and will provide any equipment you need.

Telemark Inn
✆ US (207) 836 2703
Activity packages – hiking and llama trekking from a wilderness retreat on the edge of White Mountain National Forest. Families accepted with children from 3 years.

It pays to ask

To help you connect with the best company and tour for you, you will need to ask a number of questions before you book your holiday. Ensure you give the operator detailed information about the ages, abilities and special needs of everyone in your family. In return, you need to feel assured that your family will be welcomed unreservedly. Some important questions to ask may include

▲ How many will there be in the group?

▲ Will other children be on the same trip? (If not, try to find an alternative date on which families are already booked).

▲ Have the trip guides worked with children of this age before?

▲ Do you have safety equipment to fit my child's weight and height?

▲ Can you provide children's meals?

▲ What are the toilet arrangements and how are soiled nappies dealt with?

▲ Are there any specific activities for children on the trip?

▲ How flexible is the trip itinerary?

▲ Is there any form of childcare available?

▲ Will we need to have any vaccinations?

▲ What emergency equipment does the guide carry, and where is the nearest medical facility?

Walks Worlwide
✆ UK (01332) 230883
Walking tours specifically designed for families with children of all ages. Itineraries cover northern Greece, Nepal and Morocco. More programmes are planned.

Wine Trails
✆ UK (01306) 712111
Specialize in walking holidays via vineyards, and organize individual tours with children.

Sailing

American River Touring Association
✆ US (209) 962 7873
Representing trips on five rivers in the Western USA. Welcomes children from the age of six.

AngloWelsh
✆ UK (0117) 9241200
Comfortable family canal boats from bases around the Welsh borders. Children aged 3–13 receive a special backpack.

Bridgewater Boats
✆ UK (01442) 863615
Welcome children, including babies. Full instruction and emergency service provided on traditional Victorian canal boats.

Flotilla Sailing Holidays
✆ UK (020) 8459 8787
Fleet of 99 boats set up for easy sailing in the Greek and Dalmation islands. Welcomes all ages including babies.

Minorca Sailing Holidays
✆ UK (020) 8948 2106
Childcare from four months provided seven days a week, plus special sailing tuition packages for children aged 4-plus.

Moorings
✆ UK (01227) 776677
World's largest barefoot chartering organization with a fleet of around 650 yachts.

Ocean Voyages
✆ US (45) 332 4681
Small group sailings worldwide. Family sailing sheet lists 50 yachts in 11 parts of the world, all known to welcome families. Charters can be arranged from one week to several months.

Odysseus
✆ UK (01273) 695094
European-based flotilla holidays. Good child support: they check ages of kids booked, aiming to match them with other families.

Offshore Sailing School
✆ US (941) 454 1700
Renowned schools across the US. Some offer supervised children's programmes and babysitting. Sailing tuition from the age of eight, with special half price rates.

Penelope Kellie
✆ UK (01962) 779317
Crewed charters in some of the world's more unusual destinations, including a Swallows and Amazons option in Finland.

ROW
✆ US (208) 765 0841
Rafting trips on Idaho's Salmon River, suitable for ages 5-plus. Trips generally include 3 to 5 families with child-friendly camps, schedules and menus.

Sunsail
✆ UK (01705) 222222
www.sunsail.com
Renowned shore-based resorts in Greece, Turkey and Antigua providing childcare from four months and activity clubs. Also feature UK-based children's sailing courses plus flotilla programme with some 700 yachts.

Sunworld Sailing
✆ UK (01273) 626284
Well organized shore-based resorts in Greece, Turkey and Spain offering children's clubs from 4 months plus.

Waterway Houseboat Vacations
✆ Canada (250) 836 2505
Explore undeveloped wilderness in British Columbia. Well equipped houseboats sleep 10–12, all fitted with child-resistant railings and water slides. Open to all ages.

Wolf River Canoes
✆ US (601) 452 7666
Trips ranging from a few hours to several days on a Mississippi river suitable for children of all ages.

Skiing

Adventures to the Edge
✆ US (303) 349 5219
Custom-designed family ski trips, welcoming children of all ages.

C Lazy U
✆ US (970) 887 3344
A ranch high in the Colorado Rockies, providing perfect cross-country family skiing and a comprehensive children's activity programme for two weeks at Christmas. Children accepted from three years.

Family Ski Company
✆ UK (01993) 851084
Specialist with four chalets in France. Babies accepted from new-born. Dedicated to families, providing qualified nannies, crèche, ski

and activity clubs, children's meals and babysitting.

Lotus Supertravel
✆ UK (020) 7962 9933
Quality superchalet programme operates to France, with childcare five days a week. Lots of attention to detail for families with children aged 9 months plus.

Neilson
✆ UK (0990) 994444
The big ski specialist with options throughout Canada, US and Europe. Supervised activities and clubs at some resorts only.

Powder Byrne
✆ UK (020) 8871 3300
Upmarket operator to Europe providing comprehensive Scallywags childcare from six months. Includes ski lessons in English.

Simply Ski
✆ UK (020) 8742 2541
Qualified nannies work 8.30am–5.15pm with free babysitting to midnight once weekly. Excellent childcare includes a crèche, supervised club and nannies to accompany the ski instructor, with small groups of just six children.

Ski Beat
✆ (01243) 780405
Extensive childcare provisions from three months to five years, including private nanny hire. Child discounts apply.

Ski Esprit
✆ UK (01252) 616789
www.ski-esprit.co.uk
Exclusive family skiing in France and Switzerland with outstanding childcare provisions and a Childcare Guarantee.

Ski Jaques
✆ France (4) 5054 1590/2334
skijacques@infonie.fr
Flexible ski programme, resident nanny, babysitting, children's meals plus an impressive range of baby equipment for hire.

Snowbizz
✆ UK (01778) 341455
www.snowbizz.co.uk
Offer an impressive childcare programme in France including private ski-school, qualified nannies, evening club and on-piste crèche. Babies welcome from three months.

Wildlife encounters

Abercrombie & Kent
✆ UK (020) 7559 8666
www.abercrombiekent.com
Recently introduced an Africa en Famille programme for children 5-plus. Also offers private safaris to east Africa for kids 8-plus.

African Explorations
✆ UK (01993) 822 443
Tailor-made specialist with experience of providing African safari adventures for families with young children.

Arctic Odysseys
✆ US (206) 325 1977
Itineraries aim to bring you close to whales, polar bears, seals, narwhals and caribou. Children must be aged around 12-plus. Can also plan a personal family odyssey exploring the infinite Arctic wilderness.

Baja Discovery
✆ US (619) 262 0700
Features two trips to Baja, Mexico, specifically for families with children aged 5-plus.

The Grey Whale Discovery brings you literally eye to eye with friendlies; The La Unica and Sea of Cortez trip voyages past whales, dolphins, sea lions and countless marine birds.

Big Five Tours and Expeditions

✆ US (407) 287 7995

Offers special 15-day family safaris to Kenya. Their off-the-beaten-track itinerary includes lessons in Swahili, wildlife viewing and cultural visits. No minimum age, though over 4 is recommended.

The Field Studies Council

✆ UK (01743) 850674

A range of wildlife study courses in England and Wales for children aged 10-plus.

Guerba

✆ UK (01373) 826611

Slower-paced Kenya camping safaris for families with children aged 9-plus. They include extra crew to assist with chores.

Hydroshere

✆ US (310) 230 3334

Shark expeditions in special floating cages and overnight sea lion excursions are their speciality. Welcomes children from 8-plus.

Journeys International

✆ US (734) 665 4407

www.journeys-intl.com

Offers a Kenya Active Week for families, as well as a family Tanzania Wildlife Week. Both include big game tracking and meeting local families in their tribal villages.

Natural Habitat Adventures

✆ US (303) 449 3711

Family trips, welcoming children 6. Tours range from tracking mountain gorillas in East Africa to swimming with wild dolphins in the Bahamas. Some include assisting scientists in marine research projects.

Nomad African Travel

✆ UK (01243) 373 929

www.nomadafricantravel.co.uk

Self-drive and tailor-made itineraries across Africa. Plenty of experience arranging family tours.

Okavango Tours

✆ UK (020) 8343 3283

info@okavango.com

Provide tailor-made safaris to suit families. Some safari camps restrict under-12s during peak season, but a private mobile safari (Tanzania, Botswana) welcomes families of all ages year-round. Under-2s recommended for malaria-free areas. Can cater for travellers with special needs.

Overseas Adventure Travel

✆ US (617) 876 0533

Travellers aged from 6-plus can choose between cultural encounters in the Serengeti, Costa Rica or the Galapagos Islands.

RSPB Holidays

✆ UK (0870) 601 0215

www.rspb.org.uk

Family programmes designed for members aged 6-plus. Destinations include the UK, Holland, France and Ghana. Wildlife observation combined with adventure activities.

Wildlife Worldwide

✆ UK (020) 8667 9158

Conservation minded operator offering innovative tailor-made wildlife tours worldwide. Trips can be specifically arranged to suit individual families.

Archaeology

Most of the archaeological and conservation holidays in the UK demand a minimum age of 16 for volunteers. Contact the English Tourist Board for more details.

Ancient World Tours
✆ UK (07071) 222950
Tours of historic sights to Egypt, Iran, Israel, Greece, Syria, Lebanon and Syria for families with children aged 8-plus. Some itineraries include an academic expert as well as a local guide.

Andante Travels
✆ UK (01980) 610555
Owned and run by archaeologists. Guided tours range from the deserts of Syria, to cave art in northern Spain, to the ancient civilizations of central Turkey. May take older children and teenagers with a real and committed interest in archaeology.

Dinosaur Discovery Expeditions
✆ US (970) 858 7282
Associated with a children's museum, the camp in Colorado welcomes families with children aged 6-plus. It mixes educational fun and games, digging, simulated lab work and hikes.

Earthwatch
✆ UK (01865) 311600 & US (617) 926 8200
A non-profit organization funding research projects around the globe. It brings lay participants together with researchers to work together on-site. Ages vary, but families with teenagers can often work as volunteers.

White Mountain Archaeological Center
✆ US (520) 333 5857
Family volunteers accepted from 9-plus to work on the site of a prehistoric pueblo overlooking the Little Colorado River.

Wyoming Dinosaur Center
✆ US (307) 864 2997
Families work beside palaeontologists at this genuine dig site which has unearthed one of the largest dinosaur finds in recent history. Children aged 8–13 can take part in 3-day weekend digs, which include dinosaur art classes and fossil tours.

Adventure plus

Acorn Activities
✆ UK (01432) 830083
Hotel-based, family adventure holidays in the Black Mountains, including activities from pony trekking to kayaking.

The American Camping Association
✆ US (765) 342 8456
www.acacamps.org
Huge variety of programmes, from studying marine life to model rocketry.

Canterbury Travel
✆ UK (01923) 822388
Can arrange a trip to Lapland to visit Father Christmas.

EcoSummer Expeditions
✆ US (604) 669 7741
Wilderness, adventure, teamwork, good times and making new friends are the philosophies behind these eco-family trips. Children accepted from age 3.

Manor House Activity Holidays
✆ UK (1584) 861333

Caters for families over the summer holidays. Children are grouped by age for activity sessions. Adults can choose from a range of multi-activity programmes. Babies and toddlers are welcome free of charge.

Sun Esprit
✆ UK (01252) 616789

Alpine summer holidays with a range of outdoor pursuits, qualified nannies, free babysitting and children's activity clubs.

Travelbag
✆ UK (01420) 54007
www.travelbag-adventures.co.uk

Opt for a range of family adventures including beach, sightseeing and jungle walks in Thailand, Morocco's casbahs or mountain villages, or combine a jeep safari, hike and cruise in Turkey. Groups of 3–5 families, with no under-5s.

VFB Holidays
✆ UK (01242) 240332

Action-packed holidays in the French Alps for all the family, and especially recommended for teenagers.

Specialist travel agents

The UK has been slow off the mark when it comes to offering a travel service specifically aimed at families. Not surprisingly, the US has more to offer. Some of the best agents to contact for advice include

American Wilderness Experience
✆ US (303) 444 2622

Specialists in environmentally friendly holidays. They will only represent tour operators that are ecologically minded.

Families Welcome
✆ US (541) 482 6121

Travel agency specializing in family trips.

Joanna Norris
✆ UK (020) 8788 3653

Joanna acts as a family holiday broker and plans to open a fully-fledged travel agency of her own, specializing solely in family holidays.

Jo Macgregor
✆ UK (01727) 766884
jo.macgregor@quovardistravel.co.uk

Jo's major aim in setting up her business is to understand and serve her customer's individual needs. She has one member of staff dedicated to family travel who is a parent herself and fully empathizes with any parents trying to plan a family holiday.

Pat Dickerman's
Adventure Travel Advisory Service
✆ US (602) 596 0226

Pat has been a part of the adventure travel business for several decades.

Travelling with Children
✆ US (510) 848 0929

Family-orientated travel agency that can help you with all your holiday arrangements.

further reading

Europe for the Independent Traveller, published by the RAC.
Travel with Children by Maureen Wheeler, Lonely Planet.
The Tropical Traveller by John Hatt, Penguin.

saving money

The first time you travel with children, you discover that money can melt quicker than an ice cream cone. Treats, souvenirs, long-distance phone calls and amusement arcades are only half the story. The reality is that the minor hardships that were acceptable to you as a single person often seem intolerable once you have children. Hotels with poor soundproofing, over-used mattresses and limited bathroom facilities might be cheaper, yet can also make for sleepless nights, bug bites and squabbles. Equally, bargain flights with cramped leg room, untold restrictions (no buggies, no cots, no car seats) and few provisions for children can prove highly taxing. If saving money is going to demand a heavy toll on your already waning parental resources – most notably your energy and patience – then you had better be sure it will be worth it in the long run.

even if you just move the items without warning the staff, you could end up getting charged for them).

Self-catering is not only flexible for families, but it can save you a fortune so long as you remember to stock up on all the essentials before you arrive. Closer to the attractions, you will find prices rocket, even when all you need is a humble loaf of bread. Consider taking along dry food favourites from home if Customs regulations permit.

Working holidays

Once your children are that bit older you will find there is one sure way of enjoying a holiday at little cost or even none at all. There are plenty of charities that organize conservation working holidays with no practical skills required. The type of voluntary work you may find yourself involved with could vary between taking part in an excavation, working to preserve wildlife and the environment, or restoring national treasures. Either way, far from the standard tourist trappings, it will provide you with the unique opportunity to stay in a remote community, often acquire new language skills and sometimes learn something of the customs and culture of a hidden society. Though it is usually necessary to pay a registration fee, both board and lodging are provided in most cases, or are at least heavily subsidized. Social events and excursions are invariably included in the programme. Try contacting Earthwatch worldwide for further details of their volunteer opportunities. They have offices in England, the US, Australia and Japan. You will find them at www.earthwatch.org.

contacts

British Universities Accommodation Consortium
✆ UK (0115) 950 4571

Debonair
✆ UK (0541) 500300

Earthwatch
✆ UK (01865) 311600 & US (617) 926 8200

easyJet
✆ UK (0870) 600 0000
www.lastminute.com

Flightline International (Gatwick South)
✆ UK (01293) 567777 (agents)

Global Volunteer
✆ US (651) 407 6100 & (800) 487 1074

Go Airlines
✆ UK (0845) 605 4321

The Insider's Guide to Discount Airfares
✆ UK (01935) 816747

Ryanair
✆ UK (0541) 569569

Travel Centre (Gatwick South)
✆ UK (01293) 535353 (agents)

YHA
✆ UK (01727) 845047

further reading

The Best Bargain Family Vacations in the USA by Valerie Wolf Deutsch and Laura Sutherland, St Martin's Press.
Cheap Sleeps Europe by Katie Wood, Ebury Press.
Peterson's Directory of College Accommodations (US) by Jay Norman.
The Green Travel Guide by Robert Lamb, Earthscan.

travel and transport

You may have decided where you are going and what you are going to do, holiday fever is upon you, but there is still the journey to face. Now comes the nagging doubt that children and travel do not mix. The nightmare scenario is that they will be constantly squabbling, or whining for something to eat, or throwing up, and always thinking up new and yet more irritating ways to ask 'how much longer?' Well, take heart; there are plenty of ways to mitigate disaster when you travel with children. The trick to organizing stress-free, comfortable and enjoyable travel is to plan well ahead, consider your family's needs, and have plenty of ideas up your sleeve to satisfy them.

Some basic rules for the journey

Keeping safe

Once you set off on your travels you will instinctively become more vigilant, especially in crowded and unfamiliar places. Extra precautions can make all the difference to your family's safety. Do not be afraid to introduce new disciplines. Children flourish within secure boundaries and being careful certainly won't lessen their sense of adventure. It will simply help you all feel more at ease to enjoy the experience.

The cardinal rule is never to let children lag behind and never let them out of your sight. Make sure you go last, and continually take a head count. In the event that you do get separated, encourage your children to remain in one place and wait for you to find them. It is a good idea to supply youngsters with a whistle to blow in case they lose sight of you in busy areas. A bright cap or jacket makes them much easier to spot. If you have more than one child, colour-match their clothes so that you only have to watch out for one thing. Older children may be trusted enough to explore by themselves within bounds. Even so, always establish a central, easy-to-find meeting place. Ensure your children carry identification at all times and that you have an up-to-date photograph of them too, just in case.

What to bring

There is a balance between bringing everything your children might use or want, and packing what they will actually need. In fact, given the choice, most children would probably wear the same T-shirt every day. The trick is to pack just enough to cover your needs, but not so much that you cannot carry it easily. Bear in mind that you have just two hands and one back. Invest in a set of luggage wheels for hauling backpacks and carry-on luggage through airports, train stations and bus depots, or simply for transporting goodies to the beach.

For convenience it is always worth having to hand wet-wipes, a change of clothing, toys to fiddle with, drinks and snacks, and some empty disposable bags. From around the age of three, children can normally manage these in their own rucksacks. It will keep their belongings exactly where they can find them and lighten your own load a little. Samsonite make a *Funny Face* range of colourful and innovative children's luggage, including mini pull-along suitcases with wheels. Do beware of leaving your children in charge of anything that is valuable or irreplaceable, however.

On the subject of precious items, you will know just what your child simply cannot do without on a day-to-day basis, whether it happens to be a best-loved blanket, teddy or pullover. You can reduce the chances of it being left behind by attaching a loop of elastic to the favourite item which can then fit comfortably around your child's wrist.

As for your main packing, separate a few individual outfits into plastic bags and put a name tag on the front. That way your children can simply grab a bag and dress themselves without a struggle. Remove disposable nappies from their packaging and stow them in the corners of suitcases to help cut down on luggage. To prevent leaks, pack your medicines and toiletries in re-sealable plastic bags.

I feel sick!

Feeling sick can make long journeys a problem for the whole family. Motion sickness is caused by a mismatch between what the balancing system within the ear is telling your brain and the messages that your eyes are receiving. The greater the amount of movement, the more motion sickness there is likely to be. If you are travelling by train or you are seated between the wings of a plane then you are unlikely to experience too many difficulties. A bus journey or choppy sea crossing, on the other hand, is much more likely to bring on an attack.

Try to avoid filling your children's tummies before you set off. What you see as a comforting meal may not be quite so good for your child in the long run.

Plenty of fresh air can help, as can sitting still with your eyes shut. Travelling later in the day is generally better than first thing in the morning. If you do find your child is prone to travel sickness, then it is also best to have medicines close to hand. The only drawback to anti-sickness preparations is that they need to be taken well before travelling; once your child starts to feel sick it is generally too late. If you know your child is susceptible to motion sickness then it may be worth giving them a precautionary dose of medicine 2–3 hours before you set off.

Bear in mind that many of the available medicines are antihistamine, and they often cause accompanying drowsiness. Sedating your child may be a worrying side effect and not be what you want at all. On the other hand, if your children are feeling unwell, or cranky or if you anticipate a particularly long and restless journey, then a medicine which helps them sleep may be ideal. Phenergan is often prescribed to combat travel sickness and is known to have a sedative effect. If your child is one of those that finds it difficult to sleep at all, be sure to use the medication in good time, as it may be too late otherwise and may even have the opposite effect.

Either way it is best to know beforehand just what you are giving your children and how they are likely to react. Ask your pharmacist for advice and, if you feel it is necessary, try any medicines out at home before you leave.

What to wear

Comfort is the key. Layers of uncomplicated, button-free clothing should cover all eventualities. And do make sure you are fully prepared, regardless of your destination or the type of weather you are expecting. A vest, T-shirt, sweats and a light rainproof jacket are ideal. It is certainly not worth dressing children up in anticipation of your arrival. Sticky fingers, spilt food and leaky felt-tip pens all have fewer places to go in a confined space. It would be unrealistic to expect your children to look as spotless as when you left home.

Making time

Finally leave more time than you would expect to get to airports, train stations, in fact anywhere along the way, and always allow time for things to go wrong. Trying to meet a 20-minute connection with children to hurry along is asking for trouble.

Getting there

By plane

Flying is the best choice for covering large distances. Sometimes even short distances are best covered with one domestic flight rather than a strenuous series of connections that will tax any family travelling with children. Even so, flying with children can seem like an endurance test, what with the endless queues, waiting times, and long walks from one generally uninteresting area to another. Most charter flights require that you turn up two hours before take-off, and it will take even longer if the flight is delayed or there are technical problems. Even scheduled flights prefer you to turn up at least an hour early. Fortunately there are some common-sense approaches that should help you through the worst of it.

From the time you book until the time you land, the trick to flying with children is to keep clear in your mind exactly what you want, ask for it firmly and keep on asking until you get it. First, find out what your airline is likely to provide. Airlines from more affluent countries generally offer plenty of extras to help keep your children busy. Swissair, Cathay Pacific, Air Canada, Thai Air and Qantas are particularly helpful. The sort of services they offer include designated flight attendants to care for families, imaginatively designed play-packs, organic babyfoods, special pre-cut toddler meals, children's in-flight entertainment channels and pre-allocated seats. Singapore Airlines has Nintendo games operated from individual TV screens, El Al has a designated family zone, and British Airways has a whole new programme of improvements aimed specifically at families with children. Airlines from countries with less money, meanwhile, may offer little beyond the bare minimum. Air India is a classic example.

Be sure to find out in advance just what the airline does and does not allow. That way you won't arrive feeling organized and in control, only to find your plans ruined. Some airlines allow you to take along your child's car seat and collapsible cot, some even allow buggies on board – all especially useful if your schedule involves waiting time in transit. Other airlines are unfortunately far more picky.

Both the airline you choose and the timing of the flight are likely to have a significant bearing on your stress levels. Charter flights may be generally cheaper and for some destinations may even be more convenient. The problem is that the later in the day you fly, the more likely you are to be delayed. Once a flight is held up for more than half an hour it loses its take-off slot; even the shortest hold-up in a charter plane's timetable can turn into increasingly long delays for each one of that carrier's flights set to go throughout the remainder of the day. Scheduled flights are more expensive for a reason. They always retain their precedence in the take-off order, which is just as well if you are planning to arrive before it gets dark or you need to make an important connection. Do not forget that they can still be subject to delays.

Whether a night or day flight is best may ultimately depend more on availability than on what suits you as individuals. If your children are not easy sleepers, try to opt for a daytime flight, as they are less likely to disturb other passengers. A night flight may suit children who sleep easily but be sure

shoulders and also waist straps to spread the weight around your hips, plus a means of free-standing the pack so that a sleeping child can remain undisturbed, together with a clip-on weather guard. Backpacks by Karrimor, MacPac, the Gerry Trail Blazer and Lafuma 660 are among the most comfortable, and can carry youngsters of all shapes and sizes.

Your child may take a little time to get used to the idea of a backpack but don't give up after one try. The chance to give periodic rides in a pack will make walking a far more viable option for any parent with a toddler. Though many packs are designed to carry children up to four years of age, the average two-year-old is probably as heavy as you will realistically want to carry over any significant distance.

Buggies and pushchairs are ideal for restaurants, shops and wide main streets but can sometimes prove to be more of a liability on any number of crowded, hilly, winding or otherwise uneven walkways.

Where there is no footpath at all, you will find yourself forced to the edge of the road where vehicles pass much too close for comfort with your child's face at exhaust-pipe level.

One solution to this is the innovative Apollo pushchair, which has been designed with an air filter to offer some protection from fumes, pollen and other such atmospheric pollutants, though it is rather expensive. While there are advantages to buggies and prams, the idea of struggling with a collapsed buggy, a writhing infant and a changing bag down a steep stairway might be just enough to convince you of the practicality of a hands-free means of transport.

A recent and ingenious answer to this ongoing dilemma is the backpack which converts into a pull-along stroller. Equally useful, for parents travelling with more than one youngster, is the Kiddy Board. This sturdy skateboard-type platform fits to the back axle of pushchairs, allowing room for one toddler to stand while you push.

4 years and up

Remember that children hardly ever manage to synchronize their needs. The more children you have, the more stops there are likely to be. One way to minimize endless interruptions is to have each child carry their own lightweight rucksack. Even little ones will derive a sense of self-importance from carrying their own goodies.

and the more nostalgic horse and carriage. When they run, how well they run, how many people they carry, and how frequently they stop varies considerably and is often impossible to fathom. Novel though it may seem, it is not generally safe to follow the local example of piling as many people on board as possible. Driving tests and safety regulations are instituted to save lives.

Take some books along to help identify local sights, wildlife, flora and fauna. Children love to keep records to show their friends, so get them to note down what they see and perhaps draw some keepsake pictures on the back of local postcards.

By public transport

Depending on where you are in the world you are likely to discover a variety of exotic local transport, some of which will be safer than others – anything between trucks, vans, three-wheeler automatic rickshaws

Universally the most cheap and cheerful method of getting about locally is either by bus or train. It is a great way to get a taste of the culture, especially when you find yourself on board with a chattery village ancient or even an animal or two.

Globally, buses vary considerably – some with videos, toilets and air-conditioning, others little more than a shell – yet they are often the most crowded and least comfortable form of transport. How fast you travel is anyone's guess. Buses often lurch along in such a way that you will need to hold on tight to even quite large children for the entire journey. Some may stop while passengers shop, others may almost fail to stop altogether. Proceeding uphill can even require that passengers get out and walk. If you are travelling on a particularly busy route do not even think about paying for an extra seat for your child. There is no point. Three people will inevitably squeeze into a space intended for two, whether your seats are pre-paid or not.

Just because one bus lets you off at a certain point, it does not follow that the next one will pick you up there. In some countries buses will stop anywhere for you; in others they only stop only at specific points along the way.

In developing countries, long-distance bus rides can carry additional risks. Destinations affixed to the front mean virtually nothing and fares vary according to the driver's whim or whatever scam he or she happens to have going. Observe what the locals pay and act accordingly. Knowing what to pay ahead of time and handing over the money unasked can help to eliminate being taken advantage of as a gullible tourist. Try to avoid night buses too; drivers sometimes swig back bottles of alcohol or chew coca leaves to keep themselves awake. In countries where public buses double as school buses, avoid the crush of pre-school hours too.

Where there is a choice between bus or train, take the train for the sake of comfort. But remember that well organized, systematic robbery of passengers along popular tourist routes can be a real problem whatever form of public transport you take. *See Safety* for precautions and tips while travelling around.

By taxi

In some countries, any vehicle smaller than a bus may fall under the loose category of taxi so long as it has wheels on it. Unlike their expensive US or European counterpart, taxis in many parts of the world provide inexpensive, locally based transportation where few people have cars. In many countries too, there are long-distance taxis which can cut hours off a trip. These can prove extremely useful as they are often not much more expensive than a bus and deliver you direct to the door. What is more, they will stop as often as you like and the extent of the crush will depend entirely on your own luggage, not anybody else's.

Whether you are planning a long-distance fare or not, only take taxis clearly identified with official markings and avoid any that appear to have lacked proper maintenance. Always be assertive and agree an estimated fare before you set off. Do be aware of the risks you are taking if you travel without a seat belt. It is not safe to assume that, in the event of an accident, all firms will have sufficient insurance cover. If you are a family of five or more, remember too that you may not always be able to travel in the same taxi and may need to make alternative arrangements.

contacts

Licensed London Taxis
℡ UK (020) 7253 5000
Dial a black cab.

London Black Cab Lost Property
℡ UK (020) 7833 0996

By bicycle

Cycling is a surprisingly untapped source of travel and one with many advantages. Not least among them is the fact that children on bikes are usually too busy, too active and too visually stimulated to become fractious or bored.

For that feeling of ultimate adventure, cycling is something that can be combined relatively easily with children: in a seat or trailer when younger; on their own bikes as they get older. The development of traffic-free cycling routes is helping to make this feel a good deal safer in towns. Whatever the terrain, however, practical road skills remain essential, even outside built-up areas. In some countries rules of the road and speed limits are often near to non-existent. It is therefore always wise to check out your child's road sense before you set out for the unknown.

So long as your children are old enough to cycle themselves you will find it keeps them fit, improves their coordination, offers them a sense of freedom and, of course, tires them out nicely too. Be realistic. Your choice of route will depend far more on your own personal fitness than the relative size of their legs to yours. As a rough calculation, infrequent cyclists are likely to cover between 6 and 10 miles (9–16km) per hour at a gentle pace. Those who cycle regularly should average around 10–15 miles (16–24km) per hour.

The volume and weight of equipment are limiting factors so it is important only to take along the essentials, not forgetting some spare parts and a tool kit. Helmets are important but must fit properly to be

contacts

Cyclists' Touring Group
✆ UK (01483) 417217

Specialized Bicycle Components
✆ US (408) 779 6229

Sustrans
✆ UK (0117) 929 0888

further reading

On Your Bike
✆ UK (0191) 213 2058
Quarterly family cycling magazine.
Family Cycling Trailguide by Nick Cotton, With details of 250 traffic-free cycle trails across the UK.
Mountain Bikes, Usborne. 11+
My First Bike Book by Frank Dickens, Haynes.

effective. They need to fit snugly, but comfortably, flat on top of the head, and should not be able to move easily. Otherwise specialist cycling clothing is not absolutely necessary, though plenty of drink and snacks are a must. Cut down on delays by giving each child their own water bottle.

If your children are going to be seated without pedalling, you will need to make sure they are not getting too cold. Layers of clothes are ideal and high-quality windproof and waterproof outerwear is useful for most climates. Equally, children are prone to burn before they become uncomfortably hot, so use plenty of sun protection.

Babies and toddlers

You can cycle with a child in a seat clamped behind you just as soon as they are able to hold their head up bearing the weight of a helmet. From around nine months they can be perfectly happy alternately day-napping, fiddling with their toes, humming and watching the world go by while you do all

the work. A zippable bag of toy treasures can be kept within reach for the occasional moments of monotony.

To give the best protection it is a good idea to invest in as encompassing a seat as you can find, and cover vulnerable areas such as knees, elbows and ankles. Kettler and Rhode Gear child seats are considered among the safest and most comfortable. You are unlikely to find children's bicycle seats available worldwide, however, so try to take a tried and tested model along with you. It is never worth risking poor quality. Avoid any that appear to be homemade.

Bicycle trailers of all kinds are suitable for children aged anywhere between three months to eight years, and are excellent for longer trips. Off road, though, they can prove harsh on very young children. Enclosed models that can carry at least two children include the Bike Burro Classic, Equinox Tourlite, Burley and Winchester Original. It is wise to add a flag and fluorescent stickers for greater visibility.

4–8 years

Trailer bikes provide an additional wheel, pedals, handlebar and even gears that attach to the back of an adult bike. This can prove an enjoyable and helpful addition during those tricky in-between years.

8 years and up

Children's bikes tend to be heavy to withstand mistreatment. By the time your child is ready to use gears properly, a small mountain bike or basic 10-speed model is likely to be easier to ride. The smallest standard touring bicycle has a 16-inch frame. Children can carry a scaled-down version of whatever you are carrying. Although carrying gear does affect balance and bike performance, children are said to adapt even more quickly than adults. Don't ask too much of your children though. Any hill that looks big to you will look twice as huge to a child. Slow down accordingly. When in convoy, it is always best for an adult to ride in the rear position for higher visibility.

practicalities

Holidays are a time when many people delight in being as impractical as possible, as reckless as possible and as unprepared as possible, imagining themselves to be free of ties and strife and unbound by the petty cares and concerns of everyday living. Dream on. Children bring with them responsibilities and with responsibilities come practical concerns which must be faced up to if a holiday is to be successful.

Babysitting

Some parents may look forward to a holiday as the time they will spend devoted entirely to their children. Yet for many people a holiday is a means not to spend more time with the kids but to escape from them.

The most extensive babysitting facilities are offered at large hotels and popular resorts. This may not be your first choice for a holiday, but it could make all the difference, offering you a measure of freedom. Smaller hotels may have a babysitting service available on request. Concierges can often provide lists of recommended babysitters. Others may simply offer a baby-listening service. This will still allow you to move around the hotel or visit somewhere close by while an elected member of staff listens out for any crying infants.

Tourist boards can often recommend suitable family hotels and may have details of qualified local babysitters or childcare agencies. It is also worth looking in the local equivalent of the Yellow Pages or even approaching a local hospital or school for referrals and advice.

Though qualifications are preferable, in practice all you can really do is make up your mind whether a babysitter can be trusted once she (or he) arrives. There is always likely to be a sense of uneasiness when you do not know the person well, especially if their grasp of English is not good. The most important thing to make clear is what is and is not expected (such as not allowing the children to drink the tap water, not disciplining them and not offering them snacks other than those you have left out). Rates, of course, will vary and will be largely negotiable, though it is normal practice to pay for the babysitter's transport to and from your accommodation.

Breastfeeding

If you are breastfeeding already, you will be well aware of the benefits of this portable method of nourishment. It not only guarantees babies a meal at any time but also provides a true sense of security and continuity when everything around them is changing. Happily, nursing etiquette is becoming more and more relaxed and nowadays you do not need to skulk away to a shabby bathroom to feed your baby. Most major airports, railway stations, ferries and department stores have their own mother and baby rooms.

In hot climates and underdeveloped countries, frequent feeds help to avoid dehydration and establish better immunity. Even in the hottest weather, exclusively breast-fed babies do not need anything else to drink, though they are likely to want

'And now, child,' she said, fingering the bow of her bonnet strings, 'I think we ought to see about our cabins. Keep close to me, and mind you don't slip.'

'Yes, grandma!'

'And be careful the umbrellas aren't caught in the stair rail, I saw a beautiful umbrella broken in half like that on my way over.'

'Yes, grandma.'

Katherine Mansfield – 'The Voyage'

to suckle more. It is a myth that either high temperatures or high altitude have an adverse effect on the flow of breast milk.

In the countries of Africa and southern Europe, especially, it is normal to breast-feed, though this does not mean you are at liberty to be indiscreet. Few people will be surprised at your breastfeeding, but it is not normal to see it in restaurants, for example. If in doubt, a strategically buttoned cardigan works wonders. Nursing shirts with concealed openings also offer mothers a certain degree of privacy.

One item worth taking with you is the Breast-Nurse, which consists of two soft, lightweight and discreet treatment packs, ideal for relieving the pain caused by engorgement, mastitis or weaning. Simply chill in the fridge, or warm in hot water and hey presto, instant relief.

Cots

It can be worth buying a travel cot if you plan to travel widely to places where cots are either not provided or are expensive to get hold of. For some families a travel cot may even be a better investment than a standard cot, as most have safe mesh panels and can double as a playpen. A wide variety is available, the lightest weighing about 11lbs (5kg). They all fold into reasonably compact bundles and will fit into the back of a car. Some are sturdy enough to take a child up to the age of four and all will comfortably accommodate infants up to the age of two.

Before you do splash out though, consider how often you are going to use the cot and what your priorities are. The sturdier

For EC citizens

British families staying in, or travelling through, EEA countries (the EEA consists of the EC plus Iceland, Liechtenstein and Norway) can get free or reduced cost emergency medical treatment if they have a completed E111 form. To apply for an E111, pick up the information leaflet *Health Advice for Travellers*, published by the Department of Health. The leaflet and application form are available from main post offices, Benefit Agency offices or the Health Literature Line on ✆ UK (0800) 555777. The completed form needs to be validated at the post office and, once stamped, remains valid as long as you are resident in the UK. To receive treatment abroad it is essential to produce the validated form and some form of identity, such as a passport, to prove you are a EC citizen. You often have to pay for the treatment initially, then claim your expenses back later, so you will need to keep any receipts. The E111 covers families with dependent children up to the age of 16, or 19 if they are in full-time education. The cost of bringing a person back home in the event of an illness is not covered however, so be sure to take out extra insurance cover for this eventuality.

ones are heavier and more expensive than the flimsier types, which can amount to little more than a piece of fabric suspended on a frame. Some mattresses are more substantial than others. You might want to choose a travel cot that takes a normal cot mattress for daily use.

Some of the best portable cots to look out for include Mothercare's Sleep 'n' Go, Cabrito's Luxury Travel Cot, Graco's Rollabed and the Travelite Regent Travel Cot. Expensive hotels will almost always supply cots, and many other places can provide a cot on request. If needs must, two armchairs pushed together and buffeted with blankets provide a safe, if temporary, alternative.

Electricity

Even in the safety of your own home, electricity and children just don't mix. This is still more true when you are on holiday as electricity varies globally, both in its voltage and in its efficiency. In many parts of the world accidents with electricity are common. Domestic wiring systems can be faulty or dangerously overloaded, while mains electricity poles and cables out in the street may prove just as precarious. Check for potential hazards.

Plug fittings are equally unpredictable. Plugs themselves may be round or square and appliances may have two round-pin, three round-pin, two flat-pin or three flat-pin fittings, depending on which country (or even area of a country) you are visiting. Wherever you travel you are best off taking an approved travel socket converter. These are readily available at most electrical outlets, airports and from mail-order catalogues. Across the world and in much of Europe the standard current is 220 volts AC. Do not take anything for granted though. In Australia and in many parts of Africa 240 volts AC is more commonly used. Always check before you go.

Insurance

It is essential that anyone going on holiday, overseas or otherwise, takes out adequate travel insurance to cover theft, loss and medical problems. Single-trip policies are available from most travel agents, insurance companies or post offices. You are not obliged to buy insurance from the same travel company that you book with. It can be cheaper if you do, but it always pays to check out other options. If you have children under the age of two, remember that most companies should offer free travel insurance for them as part of a parent's policy. An annual insurance policy, too, can be especially cost-effective for families with two or more older children travelling overseas twice or more each year (though beware of limits on the length of each trip, or total days travelled per year).

Most travel insurance policies cover cancellation due to illness, lost or damaged luggage, lost or stolen belongings, expenses and compensation due for accidents, emergency flights home, and compensation for delays. The most important aspect of any cover is medical insurance. You should look for cover of around £5,000,000.

For families travelling outside the EEA (and for all non-UK residents) full medical insurance is essential as medical treatment or legal claims resulting from an accident can be extremely expensive, especially in countries like the USA. You may prefer to opt for insurance that pays hospitals or doctors direct, to save you having to pay on the spot and claim your money back later. Check, too, whether your policy covers you for ambulances and repatriation for emergency treatment in your home country.

For further details on holiday insurance cover, contact the Association of British Insurers on ✆ UK (020) 7600 3333. The Insurance Ombudsman Bureau on ✆ UK (0845) 600 6666 can help mediate in any dispute over a claim. Families with special needs who are travelling often require individual types of high-premium travel insurance cover. Contact RADAR, ✆ UK (020) 7250 3222, for further details.

Bear in mind that if you pay for your holiday by credit card you may get automatic travel accident insurance and even some free medical insurance for your family, though cover varies considerably. Check with your card issuer for details.

If you opt for family cover you will need to watch out for further restrictions on those family members travelling independently of each other.

Also be aware that some travel insurance policies exclude pre-existing medical conditions and dangerous sports. Pregnancy may be excluded altogether and even where it is offered it will only be for emergency treatment and not routine tests, treatment or delivery. Medicover are one of the few companies that offer a specialist policy with comprehensive cover for almost anyone with an existing medical condition.

Language

Though the English language is not as widely spoken as some travel agents would have you believe, fluency in a foreign language is rarely essential if you are just visiting a country. Mercifully, many foreigners are sympathetic to the inevitable 'do you speak English?', though it can prove to be tiresome for locals and embarrassing for tourists before long. It is always wise to leave home armed with a few useful phrases such as 'excuse me', 'sorry', 'please', 'thank you', 'hello' and 'goodbye'. A few words can go a long way and demonstrate that you are at least making the effort. *See page 215*.

It should take very little time to familiarize yourself with the basics of a language once you arrive, even if you only plan to stay for a short time. Your children certainly won't have any problem picking up local phrases. They are unlikely to be intimidated by the challenge. Faced with a language barrier, children use a system of communication that is both natural and uninhibited; each child simply speaks his or her own language with little concern for how much is understood. To them, it simply does not matter who gets it right or wrong, so long as they get by. It can help to follow their example. If you can let go of your pride, you will communicate much more easily.

Pictures and written words can often succeed where spoken words are misunderstood completely. One good method for bridging the language gap is the *Wordless Travel Book*, published by Ten Speed Press. This ingenious little book provides a wide variety of pictures at which you point to convey the message you need to say. The idea is that, in moments of urgency, you need not be hampered by language.

A sincere wish to communicate will eventually overcome any language barrier. If all else fails, and you really find yourself in trouble, it can be a good idea to seek help from a local child, preferably over the age of seven. Nowadays, children in many countries are taught English at school.

Money

Travelling with children is not cheap and it is important to have something to fall back on in emergencies. Always carry a credit (or debit) card with you. Even if you find yourself in a situation where you have no local currency, waving your plastic at a taxi driver may be enough to persuade him to drive you to the nearest bank. Globally, VISA and MasterCard are the two most widely accepted credit cards. American Express does not always do quite as nicely as they would have us believe, not benefiting from the universal status of its main competitors.

Traveller's cheques plus two major credit cards are undoubtedly the safest and most practical forms of money to carry around with you. It is always a good idea to carry more than one card in case one is rendered inactive. This can happen when you least expect it: the magnetic strip may crack, the bank computers may go down, all sorts of other things can go wrong; so be prepared to use an alternative card.

To avoid wallets full of flashy hard currency, make withdrawals using an automated cash machine (ATM), and only change your traveller's cheques as and when you need cash. Always countersign the cheques in front of the person who is going to cash them, never in advance. Deal only with authorized agents when you exchange money or buy tickets for transport and avoid changing your money on the black market. When you do use a credit card, make sure any slips you sign have a line drawn outwards from the final digit (i.e. 2,000—) to ensure that there is no room for extra digits to be added at a later date, and always make sure that your credit card is returned to you after every transaction.

If your money (or anything else of value) is lost or stolen, you will need to report the loss immediately to the local police. Unless you keep a copy of the police report you will be unlikely to convince anyone of your circumstances and even less likely to make a credible insurance claim. After reporting your loss to the police you will need to contact the nearest agent for the company that issued your traveller's cheques, and the actual company that issued your credit card direct. They can put you in touch with their nearest local office. Replacements can often be arranged very quickly. Some credit cards can even be reprinted on-site, while you wait.

Nappies

In the course of one trip your baby will use a formidable number of nappies. Thankfully, the invention of the disposable nappy has made every parent's life a little easier, even more so for travelling. Despite the inconvenience of their bulk, it can be worth carrying enough to see you through the journey, as nothing can be worse than running out at a critical moment. Although airlines may be able to supply them, you cannot count on it. Railway stations, ferry ports and coach stations are unlikely to stock them. A good rule of thumb is one nappy per hour of your journey, plus a few extra to allow for delays.

A few must-haves

All families will have their own views on what is essential to take on journey. Wherever and whenever you go though, it is always worth having to hand wet-wipes, a full change of clothing, toys to fiddle with, drinks and snacks, plus some empty disposable bags for all sorts of eventualities. A multi-blade knife, such as the Swiss Army models, can be an absolute godsend with their tweezers, scissors, pens, toothpicks and their strange assortment of blades – including the one for taking stones out of horses' hooves. Children find them fun as toys too. Of course you never know what you are going to need until you need it but some other highly recommended, if not always obvious, travel paraphernalia you might like to consider are

- a torch
- a lighter
- a night light
- an extension cord
- a roll of sticky tape
- a net shopping bag
- moisturizing cream
- a notebook and pen
- travel socket converters
- mild soap and baby shampoo
- safety-pins, a needle and cotton
- sachets of milk, sugar, salt and pepper

- Remember a roll of nappy sacks or plastic bags to dispose of soiled nappies.
- Stow cumbersome spare nappies in the gaps between your luggage.
- A fold-up, pocket-size changing mat can help cut down on bulk and make nappy-changing easy anywhere.
- Invest in an inflatable, non-slip changing mat, which is perfect for tricky manœuvring.

Disposable nappies can be bought almost anywhere in the world, though they will often cost a good deal more than at home. If you are planning a long stay, or cannot rely on shop supplies, take a large box of nappies with you. You can treat this as just another piece of luggage. Put a label on the box and check it into the aircraft hold with your other suitcases.

If you are worried about cost, your luggage allowance or the environment, then reusable, washable nappies are a good alternative. They are inexpensive, easy to carry and non-polluting. The only drawback is finding the time to wash and dry them. If you are interested in finding out more, try any one of the growing mail-order supply companies. *See page 109* for details.

Passports

In the UK

If you are going abroad with your new baby, you will need to make sure the baby has a passport too. All babies born since 5, October 1998 now require their own travelling papers. The measure has been introduced to make it easier to identify children, and harder for unauthorized adults to sneak them out of the country. A child's passport costs £11 and is valid for five years. Children under 16 included on a parent's passport before 5, October 1998 do not require a separate passport, though they are eligible to apply for one of their

own if they want to. It is worth remembering that if your children's details are recorded on the mother's passport only, the children will have to remain with mum during check-in and the journey. If one of you has to travel home with a sick child, it will be mum that has to go home early.

For adults, the one-year British visitor's passport has been phased out and is no longer available. A full 10-year passport must now be applied for. The current cost stands at £18. A passport application form or renewal form can be obtained from any main post office. It is important to leave enough time for your application to be processed, especially if you are planning to travel during the school holidays. Ring the passport information service on ☎ UK (0990) 210410 for recorded details of current waiting times and further advice. Expect a waiting time of of at least two months. One agent who can provide a passport in as little as 24 hours is the

Social Security number, two passport-size photos and some form of identification showing a picture of you. Passports cost $40 for children under 18 and $65 for adults. It is important to leave enough time for your application to be processed, as delays of six weeks and longer are normal. You can make passport applications for children under 13 without them being

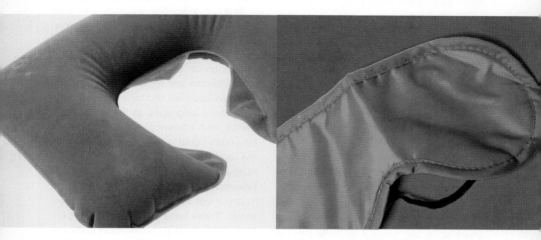

Passport Emergency Service, based in Portsmouth ☎ UK (0870) 606 2909. The agency charges £100, or £55 for a turn-around of seven days.

In the US

All US citizens, including infants, must have a passport to travel abroad (except to Canada, Mexico and some Caribbean islands). A passport application can be made at the US Passport Agency, designated post office or local courthouse. You need to take along originals or certified copies of your family's birth certificates,

present, but all children over that age need to apply in person. An adult passport is valid for 10 years. A child's passport is valid for just five. More detailed information can be accessed on the Internet at www. travel.state.gov/passport_services.html.

Sleep

Any child with established sleep patterns can find it difficult to adjust when they travel to a new place. You should be prepared for the fact that your child may not want to go to bed at the usual time or even sleep as long, and you may need to spend much more time reading books and settling them down. They may give up daytime naps altogether. Ultimately, be prepared to accept a totally new routine during your time away. If you can get your child used to sleeping in different places from an early age, then all the better. Babies can and do sleep just about everywhere, and this is the ideal time to try out different rooms at home so that they can get used to the idea of sleeping in different environments. If you have left it too late, then establishing some sense of continuity away from home will help reduce your child's sense of upheaval. When it is bedtime even young babies will develop an awareness of their immediate surroundings and will react more comfortably to something familiar. Creating a place to sleep each night with a special blanket, bottle or teddy will help give your child the same sense of security as bedtime at home.

A plug-in night light should help keep anxieties at bay while a portable bed-rail will prevent children falling out of a bed they are unfamiliar with. Both of these products are available by mail order. *See page 109* for mail-order companies.

If you are travelling late and expect to arrive at your accommodation past bedtime, try to have the children ready dressed in their pyjamas so that they can be put to bed with minimum fuss. A special, child-size travel sleeping-bag with a hood means they can be taken straight from the car to bed without any of the hassle of finding the right bedding and tucking them in.

Telephones

It's not only the lovable ET who wants to phone home. Children can often find it reassuring to ring up a friend or relation back home, just to check that home is still there. Sometimes, too, they can find it a hoot to phone such a long distance, and more immediate than a postcard.

Globally, telephone systems can vary from the superb to the dire, from the relatively cheap (Spain) to the extortionate (South Africa).

Throughout the world, modern public phone booths are often both credit card- and coin-operated and have instructions in a variety of languages. In terms of convenience and efficiency the humble public telephone booth is hard to beat, so long as the vandals have not got there first. Even in Australia's Outback you can find solar-powered, satellite-connected booths.

Watch out for overseas calls made from hotels. These have to be the most expensive way to hold a conversation known to humankind. It is normal for them to at least treble or even quadruple the call rate. Indeed you should expect to pay a big surcharge if you make any calls from a phone that does not have a coin slot. The exception is, of course, if you invest in an international telephone card before you leave home. Nowadays these are available from a number of telephone companies. In the UK, the BT Chargecard is popular; in the US, Sprint, MCI and AT&T cards are widespread. These all offer very competitive rates, especially for calls abroad. The cards provide all sorts of credit or pre-paid contacts

ABC Holiday Extras Travel Insurance
✆ UK (0800) 171000

Association of Breast Feeding Mothers
✆ UK (020) 8778 4769

Association of British Insurers
✆ UK (020) 7600 3333

Breast Nurse Packs
✆ UK (020) 7267 6110

Cabrito
✆ UK (020) 8201 0505

Childminders Babysitting Service
✆ UK (020) 7935 2049

Coping with Children's Sleep Problems
✆ UK (0151) 632 0662
New audio cassette from the Royal College of Psychiatrists.

Earthwise Baby
✆ UK (01908) 585769
Eco-friendly mail-order company.

Graco
✆ UK (0870) 909 0510

Insurance Ombudsman Bureau
✆ UK (0845) 600 6666

La Leche League
✆ UK (020) 7242 1278
Advice on breastfeeding.

Little Green Earthlets
✆ UK (01825) 71330
Washable nappies by mail order.

MEDEX Assistance Coorperation
✆ US (410) 453 6300

Medicover
✆ UK (0870) 735 3600

Mothercare
✆ UK (01923) 210210

The Passport Agency
✆ UK (0990) 210410

Perfectly Happy People
✆ UK (0870) 607 0545
Kooshies by mail order.

Posh Potty
✆ UK (029) 2057 5600
Non-spill travel potty.

Post Office Counters Services
✆ UK (0345) 223344

Post Office Travel Insurance
✆ UK (0800) 387858

Sam-I-Am
✆ UK (020) 8995 9204
Mail-order cotton nappies.

Snugger
✆ UK (020) 8224 8766
Mail-order infant sleeping-bags.

Snuggle Naps
✆ UK (0115) 953 6604
Mail-order washable, designer nappies.

Travel Insurance Direct
✆ UK (0161) 962 5570

Worldcover Direct
✆ UK (0800) 365121

further reading

The Bathroom Survival Guide by Eva Newman, Marlor Press.
Sleep and the Traveler, available from the National Sleep Foundation at 7758 Sunset Boulevard, Los Angeles, California, USA.
The Wordless Travel Book by Jonathon Meader, Ten Speed Press.

packages to suit you and normally come with full instructions and security pin numbers. The standard procedure is to dial a designated freephone number and ask for the English-speaking operator to connect you. It is certainly much easier than juggling a handful of foreign coins.

Most cities and tourist resorts also have a central telephone bank where you can check the phone directories and make calls from a metered booth. There is a strong temptation to get carried away when you are seated in comfort without having to feed the slot. While they are practical, they are also quite costly (though indispensable for making reverse charge or collect calls). Make sure you only use telephone offices that look official and businesslike. Unscrupulous fax and phone bureaus can end up costing a fortune.

Bear in mind that telephone sockets, like plug sockets, are not universal and vary in size throughout the world and even across a continent, as with Europe. If you have a portable laptop computer and intend to rely on a telephone socket for a connection to your modem, be sure to buy an adaptor kit before you leave home. Both Xircom and Targus make portable sets to keep you on-line wherever you are.

Tipping

This is an accepted part of everyday life in many countries. Though a voluntary gratuity is usually associated with performance and service, it is just as often taken for granted. On cruise ships and at fancy hotels tipping falls just short of mandatory. Many people who work in the leisure industry are underpaid and depend on tips as a major part of their wage so don't be stingy. Waiters and tour guides, for example, only make a decent living if they receive decent tips. If you do not give a tip, there is always a chance things will turn nasty. You should always tip whenever you feel it seems appropriate.

Some tips are built into the pricing structure and are included on your bill. Many restaurants automatically add a service charge and even add on a 'suggested tip' to their bills. Keep a beady eye out for these extras. It is also a good idea to check beforehand for attitudes towards tipping in the country you are visiting. Brochures, guidebooks and consulates should be able to tell you more. It is important to remember that what you intend as a measure of your gratitude can be seen as an insult in some cultures. Some resorts, too, have a strict policy of no tipping. If in doubt, ask.

Toilets

Some children are fascinated by unfamiliar toilets; others may feel intimidated by them. If you know you are going to be travelling in the near future, encourage your children to get used to new toilets when you are out and about in places they are more accustomed to (such as shops, friend's houses and restaurants).

Toilets abroad differ not only in shape and size, but invariably in their states of cleanliness. You will encounter anything from chic, coin-operated kiosks that self-disinfect, to daunting holes in the ground. Standards of hygiene can sometimes be considerably lower than you may be used to as well. This is especially the case when you travel off the traditional tourist path into more remote and economically under-developed regions. You might want to carry a spray bottle of diluted bleach (1:10 with water). This is always useful for spraying public toilet seats before little hands reach out to the germs. You should also make sure you are armed with spare toilet roll or an equivalent, as toilet paper may be non-existent. In some places you may even be asked to pay for it.

The snazzy *Posh Potty* is a lightweight, spill-proof potty with a lid, which is ideal for younger travellers. For those that have progressed, take along a portable potty seat or toilet adaptor. Some fold up small enough to fit inside a handbag. Disposable toilet seat covers are also a good idea for older kids, not to mention adults.

If a public toilet is not close to hand, most restaurants, hotels or bars will happily oblige if you explain your need. There is every likelihood that these will be a good deal cleaner. Fast food joints are always a safe bet. In an emergency, you can let a little boy use a jar or cup, or whatever else comes to hand, or try placing something absorbent – like a disposable nappy or tissues – into a plastic bag.

Do not get upset if your toddler regresses temporarily and you need to revert back to nappies for a while. Try to be patient and understanding. You can get back on track once you return home. If you think you might have a problem, pack a waterproof-backed bedsheet just in case.

Visas

Children with their own passports require their own visas too, but a child included on a parent's passport normally does not (though some countries will demand that visas are stamped separately, even if the child is travelling on your passport). This can result in considerable savings, as visas are often far from cheap.

A number of countries still require official entry visas. Visa applications should be directed to the relevant embassy or consulate of the country you plan to visit. You will need to have an up-to-date passport and a photograph. It may take a month or more to obtain a visa, so be sure to apply in good time. If you are in a particular hurry, special arrangements can sometimes be made providing you have evidence of your travel dates.

The British Passport Office only handles visa entry applications on behalf of remaining British dependent territories, such as Bermuda, Barbados and Gibraltar. For these visa enquiries you can contact the Passport Office on ✆ UK (020) 7271 8552.

US citizens can find out more about visa application at www.travel.state.gov/visa_services.html, or by contacting the Visa Services Inquiries Branch on ✆ (202) 663 1225, which offers a telephone helpline.

staying away from home

The first decision most families make when planning a holiday is where to go. This is obviously important, but no more so than finding the right place to stay. No matter how ideal your destination is, you will be disappointed if your accommodation is awful or not what you expected. Thankfully, the options of where to stay on a family holiday are practically limitless nowadays. As well as the standard villas, pensions, hotels and apartments you find a whole range of accommodation to cater for every taste. There is everything from restored mansions and paradores to igloos, rice boat houses and log cabins. You can even stay in a gypsy cave.

Hotels and hotel chains

If you want some privacy you can choose to be miles from anywhere, in the middle of a forest, on a cliff-top or on a private desert island. If you like the thought of having other families around, you can opt for a family resort with on-site swimming pools, playgrounds, restaurants, bars, entertainment and, most importantly, other children for your brood to hang around with.

Of course no one place is likely to prove perfect for every member of your family. Before you make a final decision, it is best to consider the pros and cons of different types of accommodation.

When you are looking for a place that suits you best, you need to weigh up

- cost
- facilities
- local amenities
- space
- privacy

Once you have a good idea of what you are looking for, making the right choice becomes much easier.

Hotels

Thankfully, the days when children were neither seen nor heard – let alone welcomed – on the premises of most hotels are fading fast. In the past, hotels were never exactly noted for their child-friendliness. The pursed lips, almost inaudible tuts and can't-you-control-your-child looks were too much to bear. Now, however, more and more are following Spain and Italy's legendary tolerance of children and specializing in family holidays. Increasingly, those who say they welcome children actually mean it, and it is now quite normal to see well equipped and supervised nurseries, qualified staff, organized activities, baby-listening and children's TV channels.

Despite the added pros, though, the cons of choosing to stay in a hotel remain the same. You may be expected to fit in with the hotel's other child-free clients, but there is no guarantee your baby or toddler will oblige. Children do not like being restricted at the best of times, still less do they tolerate hushed spaces, specific mealtimes, set menus and unfamiliar foods.

If it all seems too stressful, request the rooms at the end of a hall. That way, you will have less worry about the extra noise your kids are certain to make. If your concerns are more about the noise outside, in a busy resort or city centre for example, insist on a courtyard room or one towards the back of the hotel.

As for contented mealtimes, look out for hotels that provide children's menus, separate children's tea times and evening babysitting. Such services can save lives!

Bear in mind, too, that hotel childcare, useful though it is, rarely offers cover for parents to leave the premises. You are best off finding a hotel that not only caters for children but provides plenty for the adults to do as well.

What to expect for your money

Many countries worldwide use a star system to rate their hotels. A 1- to 5-star plus rating depends on the facilities available. You will often find the number of stars earned displayed prominently near the front door. If it is not clear, ask.

Though star ratings correlate closely with price, they sometimes have little to do with the cleanliness, appearance or overall atmosphere of the accommodation. An immaculate but no-frills hotel with few amenities may still be far more inviting than a characterless, middle-of-the-road 3-star hotel, despite the latter boasting its own in-house restaurant and cable TV.

The term 'double room' can mean one of an assortment of features, depending on which part of the globe you are visiting. In the UK and France you will normally be offered a room with one double bed, in Spain a room with two single beds, while in the USA it is normal to expect two double beds when you book a double room. Ask when you make your booking.

For families, a junior suite usually comprises a bedroom, a small lounge and a bathroom. Another option is to book two interconnecting rooms, with just a door dividing you. In the US, all-suite hotels are popular and make sound financial sense.

One important thing to bear in mind is that if you choose a budget hotel room, especially outside the US, it is likely to mean just that. There will probably be little more than the bare basics, and often not even a television.

Costs

If cutting costs is a priority, book a room in which your children can stay for nothing. There are usually discounts for children under 12 and often free deals for the under-4s and -5s. Discounts are usually based on two adults travelling together, however, and

some involve children sleeping in a room with the adults.

If you end up having to sleep in the same room as your children, make sure there is somewhere for you to relax without disturbing them. Some countries have gone so far

Are you welcome?

Decide what is most important to you, then speak to the agent or hotel direct and ask all the relevant questions. It is not just the facilities that matter, but a relaxed, child-friendly attitude, which could make all the difference to your family holiday. Simply providing a cot is not enough to make a family feel welcome. In particular, look out for

- Special family packages or discounts
- Children's menus
- Either separate children's meal times or a policy of not excluding children from the restaurant
- Available babysitters or baby-listening
- A crèche or a supervised children's programme
- Activities especially aimed at families
- Availability of books, games and toys for children
- Qualified childcare staff
- A friendly atmosphere that is welcoming to children
- Quality cots

as to install a national pricing policy for families. In Portugal, for example, children under eight are automatically entitled to a discount of 50 percent in any hotel if they share a room with the adult accompanying them. In the USA you are charged per room, rather than per person. Since most hotel and motel rooms have two large king-sized beds this can work out cheap so long as you do not mind bunking in together.

Hotel chains

One way of ensuring you get good facilities is to choose a hotel chain that has a policy of welcoming families. Free offers and discounts are common, though these may be restricted to weekends or off-season breaks. Hotel chains often have special concessions, activity programmes and children's menus in their restaurants. Babysitting, baby-listening, cots and high chairs often come as standard.

It is always worth contacting national tourist offices to check whether they have details of any recommended hotel chains with special schemes for visitors. Chains across the world with some of the best offers for families include

In the UK

Stakis
✆ UK (0990) 909090
Mainly 4-star hotels throughout England, Scotland and Ireland.

Swallow Hotels
✆ UK (0645) 404404
Nearly 40 hotels in England and Scotland, ranging from 3- to 5-star places.

Across Europe

Campanile
✆ UK (020) 8569 6969
www.campanile.fr
Nearly 400 hotels in seven European countries, the largest number in France.

Choice Hotels
✆ UK (0800) 444444 & US (800) 654 6200
A group of 4-star Clarion, 3-star Quality Hotels and 2-star Comfort Inns across Europe, mainly in cities close to main routes.

The Circle
✆ UK (01865) 875888
A group of individually run hotels in France, Italy, Belgium and the UK. All members are obliged to offer a child-friendly service.

Queens Moat House Hotels
✆ UK (0645) 213214
A group of 3-, 4- and 5-star hotels in the UK, Germany and the Netherlands.

Worldwide

Best Western
✆ UK (0345) 747474 & US (800) 528 1234
Some 4,000 hotels, mainly 3- to 4-star, in 78 countries worldwide. Almost 400 are in the UK alone.

Canadian Pacific Hotels
✆ UK (0500) 303030 & US (800) 441 1414
Offer services for children to make them feel valued guests. Children's own check-in area, welcome package, registration form and kids menu add to the appeal.

Days Inns
✆ US (800) 325 2525
Inns across the USA, offering Family Fun Rates and a Kids Stay and Eat Free programme.

Forte
✆ UK (0345) 404040 & US (800) 543 4300
A group including 80-plus UK Posthouse Hotels, UK based Heritage hotels, plus 100 or so 5-star Le Meridien Hotels and Resorts worldwide.

Four Seasons
✆ UK (0800) 526648 & US (800) 268 6282
A global network of 5-star hotels and resort

properties. Most hotels offer an innovative Kids for All Seasons children's programme.

Holiday Inn
✆ UK (0800) 897121 & US (800) 465 4329
A group of 2,300 hotels in more than 60 countries worldwide. Its Kidsuites and enter-tainment programmes are a big draw.

Hilton
✆ UK (0990) 445 866 & US (310) 205 4599
Boasts over 400 hotels in 50 countries, half of them in the USA. Family programmes fea-ture strongly, sometimes with welcome gifts and supervised programmes.

Howard Johnson
✆ US (800) 654 2000
A franchise group of 550 hotels and inns worldwide, principally in the USA but also Canada and Mexico. Their Kids Go HoJo programme is renowned.

Hyatt
✆ UK (0345) 581666 & US (800) 233 1234
A US group of 189 5-star hotels, primarily in North America and the Caribbean. A Camp Hyatt educational activity programme is offered at its resort hotels. Concessions apply throughout.

Loews
✆ US (800) 23-LOEWS & (212) 521 2000
US-based chain offering a wide range of child-friendly options.

Marriott Hotels
✆ UK (0800) 221222 & US (800) 228 9290
Around 1,750 hotels worldwide. Family packages are offered at most resort properties.

Mercure
✆ UK (020) 8283 4580 & US (212) 286 0664
Hotels throughout Europe (mainly France), plus Australia, Asia, the Middle East and Africa.

Novotel
✆ UK (020) 8283 4530 & US (800) 668 6835
Over 300 3- and 4-star hotels worldwide, with many in France. A special family charter makes it one of the most welcoming chains.

Radisson-SAS
✆ UK (0800) 374411& US (800) 333 3333
Over 400 5-star hotels in Europe, the Middle East and Malaysia, plus some 200 in the USA. Many feature children's programmes.

Rafael Hotels
✆ UK (0800) 181123 & US (401) 854 6795
A group of seven 5-star hotels based in
Europe and one in Florida. Represented by
the Leading Hotels of the World.

Small Luxury Hotels of the World
✆ UK (0800) 964470 & US (800) 525 4800
A collection of elegant hotels worldwide
stretching as far as Cambodia. Many
actively welcome children.

Sofitel
✆ UK (020) 8283 4570 & US (800) 221 4542
Over 100 4-star hotels sprinkled across 43
countries throughout Europe, Asia, Africa,
South America and the USA. Sofitel has a
dedicated policy of welcoming children.

Sol Melia Hotels
✆ UK (020) 7375 2121
& US (1) 800 33 MELIA
The leading hotel group in Spain, boasting
252 city and resort hotels in 26 countries
worldwide. The company supports a child-
friendly programme.

Sun International
✆ UK (01491) 411222 & US (800) 321
Some 3,000 distinctive luxury resorts in the
Bahamas, South Africa, Mauritius and the
Indian Ocean, each offering an array of serv-
ices, amenities and fun activities for families.

Westin Hotels and Resorts
✆ UK (0800) 282565 & US (800) 228 3000
More than 100 5-star hotels and resorts in
23 countries worldwide, a large number in
the US and Canada. One of the best chains
geared up to children's needs with its Kids
Club programme.

Independent hotels

There are too many independent hotels to
list comprehensively, so the priority in com-
piling this list has been naming hotels that
go out of their way to welcome children,
with minimum restrictions.

In the UK

Babington House
Somerset, England
✆ UK (01373) 812226

Baile-na-Cille
Timsgarry, Scotland
✆ UK (01851) 471121

Bedruthan Steps Hotel
Cornwall, England
✆ UK (01637) 860555

Bonham
Edinburgh, Scotland
✆ UK (0131) 226 6050

Burleigh Court
Gloucestershire, England
✆ UK (01453) 883804

Calcot Manor
Gloucestershire, England
✆ UK (01666) 890391

Ettington Park
Alderminster, Warwickshire, England
✆ UK (01789) 450123

Fawsley Hall
Bedfordshire, England
✆ UK (01327) 892000

The Gara Rock Hotel
South Devon, England
✆ UK (01548) 842342

Hambleton Hall
Oakham, Rutland, England
✆UK (01572) 756991

Hotel Continental
Kent, England
✆ UK (01227) 280280

Howard's House
Teffont Evias, Wiltshire, England
✆ UK (01722) 716392

Moonfleet Manor
Weymouth, Dorset, England
✆ UK (01305) 786948

Myhotel
Bloomsbury, London, England
✆ UK (020) 7667 6000

Old Bell
Malmesbury, England
✆ UK (01666) 822344

Porth Tocyn Hotel
Abersoch, Wales
✆ UK (01758) 713303

Runnymede Hotel and Spa
Surrey, England
✆ UK (01784) 436171

Seaview Hotel
Isle of Wight
✆ UK (01983) 612711

Stapleford Park
Leicestershire, England
✆ UK (01572) 787522

Thurlestone Hotel
South Devon, England
✆ UK (01548) 560382

Titchwell Manor Hotel
Brancaster, Norfolk, England
✆ UK (01485) 210221

Trevelgue Hotel
Porth, Cornwall, England
✆ UK (01637) 872864

Waterside Inn
Aberdeenshire, Scotland
✆ UK (01779) 471121

Woolley Grange
Bradford-on-Avon, England
✆ (01225) 864705

Wringford Down
Cawsand, Cornwall, England
✆ UK (01752) 822287

Worldwide

Albergo Miranda Da Oreste
Bergamo, Italy
✆ Italy (3) 598 6021

Casuarina Beach Club
Barbados
✆ Barbados (246) 428 3600

Cenobio dei Dogi
Camogli, Italy
✆ Italy (0185) 7241

Europe Hotel
Interlaken, Switzerland
✆ Switzerland (33) 822 7141

Hotel Aigua Blava
Costa Brava, Spain
✆ Spain (97) 262 2058

Hotel Eden
Arosa, Switzerland
✆ UK (81) 378 7100

Hotel Gruner Baum
Badgastein, Austria
✆ Austria (6434) 25160

Kelly's Resort Hotel
Rosslare, Republic of Ireland
✆ Ireland (53) 533 2114

Le Diana
Carnac, Brittany, France
✆ France (2) 97 520538

Paihia Beach Resort Hotel
Bay of Islands, New Zealand
✆ New Zealand (9) 402 6026

Paphos Amathus Hotel
Paphos, Cyprus
✆ Cyprus (6) 264300

Paradis
Mauritius
✆ Mauritius (230) 450 5070

Ripa All Suites Hotel
Rome, Italy
✆ Italy (06) 58611

Roundwood House
County Laois, Republic of Ireland
✆ Ireland (53) 50232120

Luxury Hotels

Recommended 5-star luxury hotels where children are made to feel especially welcome include

In the UK

Cliveden
Berkshire, England
✆ UK (01628) 668561

Gleneagles
Perthshire, Scotland
✆ UK (0800) 704705

Le Manoir aux Quat' Saisons
Oxfordshire, England
✆ UK (01844) 278881

Worldwide

Coral Beach Hotel
Coral Beach, Cyprus
✆ Cyprus (6) 621711

Coral Reef Club
Barbados
✆ Barbados (246) 422 2371

Datai Hotel
Langkawi, Malaysia
✆ Malaysia (4) 959 2500

Fontainebleau Hilton
Miami, Florida, USA
✆ US (505) 538 2000

Four Seasons
Boston, USA
✆ US (617) 338 4400

Glitter Bay
Barbados
✆ Barbados (246) 422 4111

Grand Hotel Villa Serbelloni
Bellagio, Lake Como, Italy
✆ Italy (031) 950216

The Hard Rock Hotel
Las Vegas, USA
✆ US (702) 693 5000

Hotel Pulitzer
Amsterdam, Holland
✆ Netherlands (20) 523 5235

Hotel Quinta Do Lago
Algarve, Portugal
✆ Portugal (89) 396666

Little Dix Bay Hotel
Virgin Gorda
✆ British Virgin Islands (284) 495 5555

Malliouhana Hotel
Anguilla
✆ British West Indies (264) 497 6111

Mandarin Oriental Hotel
Singapore
✆ Singapore (65) 338 0066

The Parkroyal
Penang, Malaysia
✆ Malaysia (4) 881 2448

The Phoenician
Arizona, USA
✆ US (602) 941 8200

The Pierre
New York, USA
✆ US (212) 838 8000

Ritz-Carlton
Denpasar, Bali
✆ Bali (361) 702222

Sheraton Mirage
Port Douglas, Australia
✆ Australia (7) 4099 5888

All-suite hotels

Similar in approach to aparthotels (which, as their name suggests, are a cross between an apartment and a hotel) all-suite hotels have really taken off, especially in the USA. These offer private sleeping areas and kitchen facilities, intended both to save money and to accommodate any kid's impetuous eating habits. The benefits are apparent. This kind of sensitivity to the special needs of both parents and children extends to the services that many of these all-suite hotels offer, including equipment rental, babysitting, play areas, on-site shops and special family packages. Some of the best for families include

Embassy Suites
✆ US (800) 362 2779
www.embassy-suites.com

Guest Quarters
✆ US (800) 424 2900

Homewood Suites
✆ US (407) 396 2229

Summerfield Suites Hotel
✆ US (800) 833 4353

Booking your hotel

If you want to find out more about a particular hotel either featured here or in a tour operator's brochure, then ring direct or ask a UK travel agent to look it up in their Agent's Hotel Gazetteer or OAG Worldwide Hotel Guide (which should be stashed somewhere under the desk). You can, of course, book through any hotel direct, but there are also a number of hotel booking agents who can help you sift through the various options.

Room Service
✆ UK (020) 7636 6888
For Italy, Spain, France and Portugal.

Hotel Promotion Services
✆ UK 0181 446 0126
For Europe and the USA.

Hotel Reservation Network
✆ US (800) 964 6835
www.hoteldiscounts.com

Quickbook
✆ US (800) 789 9887

Central Reservation Service
✆ US (407) 740 6442 & (800) 548 3311

Bed and breakfast

One of the alternatives to staying in a hotel is to opt for a small guest house or private bed and breakfast accommodation. This is often not only cheaper than a hotel, but also offers you a chance to eat home-cooked food and to get a glimpse of real home life.

Bed and breakfasts certainly put you in more direct contact with the people and places you go to see, but they can also have their own distinct drawbacks. The typical decor is not exactly child-orientated and sometimes, especially in the United Kingdom, it can verge on the downright tacky. Walls are unlikely to be sound-proofed. What is more, expensive furnishings and breakable knick-knacks may be the rule rather than the exception. Proprietors may not be keen on kids running around the property all day. In the USA, moreover, bed and breakfasts rarely accept children under the age of eight. If you want a hassle-free stay, be sure to find a place that not only accepts children, but actively welcomes them. Ask whether

❁ There are cots and high chairs

❁ It is possible to make separate children's meals at a time that suits them

❁ The children are expected to eat with the adults or at separate tables

❁ There is running around space for children

❁ There is a comfortable lounge for the adults once the children have gone to bed

Farmhouses offering bed and breakfast are often the best option with a young family as there is usually plenty to see.

Booking your B&B

There are a wealth of regularly updated books, CD software and websites that list specific bed and breakfasts worldwide. This is probably your best bet, since travel agents are not often much help when it comes to booking this type of accommodation. You will need to be prepared to do some research of your own but there are a number of specialist booking agents who can help.

In the UK

Uptown Reservations
✆ UK (020) 7351 3445
For Central London.

Bed and Breakfast (GB)
✆ UK (01491) 578803

Bed and Breakfast Nationwide
✆ UK (01255) 831235

Discover Britain Holidays
✆ UK (01905) 613 7464

Hotel and Guest Service
✆ UK (020) 7385 9922

Knights in Britain
✆ UK (01747) 820574

Worldwide

**Alberta Gem's B&B
and Reservation Agency**
✆ Canada (403) 434 6098

**AUSRES
Australian Reservation Service**
✆ Australia (3) 9696 0422

**Australia and New Zealand's
Finest B&Bs and Rural Retreats**
✆ Australia (3) 9534 2683

Self-catering

Hotels and bed and breakfasts are not always the best solution for families on the go. While you may find you need more living space, you may not be able to afford the luxury of two adjoining hotel rooms or a suite. What is more, despite some notable exceptions, too few hotels are renowned for their sympathetic or tolerant attitude towards boisterous youngsters.

On the whole, a self-catering holiday is a cheaper and more flexible option than staying in a hotel. More importantly, it offers you freedom to do what you like when you like for the duration of your holiday. You can get up at an unsocial hour, nurse your colicky newborn at 3am, scramble eggs when your toddler gets peckish, and generally make as much noise as you want or need to. At the day's end, you always have a relaxing home from home to return to without any of the added fuss of meeting hotel timetables or getting organized for set mealtimes.

At first glance, of course, self-catering may not seem like much of a holiday from the familiar domestic chores. As soon as someone mentions the cooker and kitchen sink, it conjures up images of a home routine you are desperate to escape. The reality is that you can always eat out and you need only use the kitchen for the odd meal such as breakfast and preparing impromptu snacks. It is certainly a much easier way to cope with fussy eaters.

Self-catering does not have to mean slumming it either. Far from it. Properties vary enormously and you can choose right across the board, from a simple log cabin in Sweden to an exclusive villa in the Caribbean complete with its own butler, maid, nanny and gardener.

Bed and Breakfast (Amsterdam)
✆ The Netherlands (20) 615 7527

Bed and Breakfast (Australia)
✆ Australia (2) 9498 5344

Bed and Breakfast (France)
✆ UK (01491) 578803

Bed and Breakfast (South Africa)
✆ UK (01787) 228494

Czechbook
✆ UK (01503) 240629

Finnish Country Holidays
✆ Finland (9) 5766 3300

Friends with Friends
✆ Italy (06) 3383 990

Heritage Tasmania
✆ Australia (3) 6224 1612

Hidden Ireland (Dublin)
✆ Republic of Ireland (1) 662 7166

The Italian Connection
✆ UK (020) 7486 6890

Ireland Reservations Direct
✆ UK (0800) 777377

Portfolio Bed and Breakfast Collection
✆ South Africa (11) 880 344

What to expect for your money

This kind of holiday is getting popular for short breaks and for large family reunions. In fact, many of the self-catering packages offer the best deals for families. Not only are there free offers available throughout the year, but operators are usually more generous with their upper limit on children's ages. Generous discounts for children up to the age of 16 are common (rather than the standard age limit of 11 or 12). Also, holiday costs are normally based on rental of the entire property, no matter how many people you take along, so the more of you that travel together, the cheaper it will be.

The most important thing is to find out exactly what you are getting for your money. To avoid disappointment or a row, check out as much as possible in advance, so you will know what to expect.

The standard of furnishing and equipment will obviously vary from property to property. Simple, clean, but sparsely furnished accommodation is about as much as you can expect from a gîte in France or a budget-priced, multi-storey apartment block at a resort.

Equally though, many self-catering rentals are well furnished and kitted out with libraries, music systems, board games and videos. There is no reason why you should not expect a dishwasher, microwave oven, fridge freezer, food processor, washing machine and tumble dryer. A welcome pack of groceries is often supplied to tide you over for the first 24 hours.

Ultimately, of course, it all comes down to priorities and personal choice. If you want a place with character you may well have to forgo a few luxuries.

What to look out for

Brochure descriptions are notoriously vague or misleading: read the small print carefully. Most seem to be informative, but it is always worth trying to find out what may have been conveniently omitted.

What constitutes a 'villa', for example? Usually villas are detached properties in their own grounds, but not always. 'Villa' can refer to part of a house divided up into separate units. Increasingly, the term refers to a terraced property in a purpose-built holiday village. A 'studio' normally refers to just one room, with a sofa that converts into a bed and cooking facilities in one corner.

Location

Before you book, check how far your accommodation is from the nearest shops, supermarket, restaurants, bus stop, launderette or beach, and whether access to any of them is along a busy road or down steep steps. Find out whether you are likely to need a hire car. A 20-minute walk may be fine for an adult but it is far less manageable with a baby and a toddler.

Ask about the views too. If the brochure only shows a picture of the interior, there is a good chance there's nothing much worth looking at outside.

Beds

It is important to check how many bedrooms (rather than beds) the accommodation has. The term 'sleeps six' can be ambiguous (sleeps them where?). You cannot assume 'sleeps six' means your accommodation will have three bedrooms. Often you will find that a sofa in the living room converts into a bed. You may even find you need to rearrange the room to create enough sleeping space.

Be sure to ask whether cots are supplied and if there is an additional charge for them. Ask whether the children's rooms are fitted out with bunk beds and, if so, whether these have safety rails. It is also a good idea to check out the layout of the property. Ask where the bathroom is in relation to your child's bedroom, how steep the stairs are and whether these, too, have stair gates.

Linens

Check how often fresh linen is supplied, and whether the term linen includes towels. What about tea towels?

Equipment

In particular you will need to find out whether there are high chairs, games, toys, beach equipment, a washing machine, stereo, TV and video (and whether any machines are battery- or coin-operated). Check whether you will need to take a can opener, corkscrew, cups or a sharp knife. If in doubt, ask for a full inventory. Bear in mind that although some of these may be up to local safety standards, they may not meet your own standards of safety.

Safety

Ask whether the garden or pool is fenced off and if there are any ponds, streams, cliffs or other such likely hazards. Find out whether the property is considered safe enough for children to play unsupervised. Check whether there are any open fires and whether they have fireguards. Ask, too, about tiled and marble floors. You won't get

a moment's rest if you continually have to watch your child teetering on the edges of danger.

Swimming pool

If there is a pool, find out what size it is. Ask whether there is a shallow end. Check, too, whether the pool is filtered and how often the filter is checked. If the pool is shared, get some idea of how many people use it. Peak summertime use can strain even the most efficient filtration unit.

Fuel and heating

Ask about gas and electricity supplies. Is usage included in the rent? If not, how is it paid for? Sometimes fuel is metered, or a charge may be levied at the end of your stay. If gas and electricity are charged by a meter, check beforehand how much the cost is per unit, and what sort of coins you will need to feed it.

Cleaning

Find out whether the rent includes cleaning. If so, how often is the property cleaned? It helps to find out what the weekly refuse policy is too. There is often very little point putting out bags of household rubbish and waiting impatiently for collection day as stray cats and ants run riot in your refuse. In most parts of Spain, for example, each household is responsible for disposing of its own litter in the central *basura* banks.

Babysitting

Ask whether babysitting can be arranged locally. If so, what amount of notice is required? Find out how much it is likely to cost, and whether the babysitter will speak any English.

Checking in

Be absolutely clear about directions to the property, especially if you are driving. Some of the most interesting holiday properties get their charm from being set off the beaten track. That same sense of rustic solitude may rapidly lose its lustre once it starts getting dark and you have a fractious family stuck in the back of a car. If you are considering a fly-drive option, find out what happens if your flight is delayed. Find out where any hire companies involved plan to leave your keys and documents once their offices are closed.

Be sure to confirm the exact changeover dates and times too. There is very little point driving through all through the night, only to arrive first thing in the morning to be told you cannot enter your property until mid-afternoon.

Find out who to call

Don't expect all places to operate with the same precision you may be accustomed to at home. Whatever property you book, be clear about how, where, and during what hours you can contact someone if there are problems. This might be the agent you booked with, a local representative or the owners themselves. Whoever it is, always keep their contact number to hand.

Booking your property

Almost all the larger family tour operators offer a selection of self-catering properties. Sometimes these are featured in their own dedicated brochure; often they are sprinkled throughout the operator's main holiday brochure, divided by destination.

You can either choose your property through an agency or rent privately through the small ads and web sites. The advantage of booking through an agency (especially a smaller one) is that they are likely to know and vet all their properties carefully so they are in a better position to discuss options. The disadvantage of making the booking yourself is that you will have to take what is said about the accommodation on trust and there is rarely any guarantee of quality. With an agency, at least, the property will have been properly inspected.

Whoever you book through should be able to report on availability of appropriate activities for children of different ages, and the suitability of the location for any children playing unsupervised.

Some of the best family self-catering options are listed here, including independent properties and a few tour operators that are less well known.

In the UK

Bruern Stable Cottages

℡ UK (01993) 830415

Set in the heart of England's Cotswold countryside, cottages come fully equipped, and include a games room and both an open fire and central heating. A welcome pack includes preserves made by the owner's chef. A home delivery shopping list comes with the booking form. Deliveries of newspapers and milk, even cleaning, can all be arranged.

Combermere Abbey

℡ UK (01948) 871637

An 850-year-old estate in Shropshire offering 10 stable-block cottages for rent. At Easter and in the summer months a week's holiday can include three days of supervised activity for 5–14 year olds. Babysitting, cots, high chairs and stairgates are all offered.

Coombe Mill

✆ UK (01208) 850344

Both children and pets are cherished at Mark and Pippa's Cornwall-based country cottages and riverside cabins. There are animals to feed and large grounds to roam. The centre can provide cots, high chairs, fireguards and stairgates. Babysitting is planned.

Ecosse Unique

✆ UK (01835) 870779

Particularly recommended because of its first-hand knowledge of Scotland, the agency offers a range of self-catering properties from the most basic to a clan chief's castle. Some offer child play areas and babysitting. Most have a selection of games.

Landmark Trust

✆ UK (01628) 825925

The Landmark Trust is dedicated to finding and refurbishing properties of character and history. They have a wide range of unusual properties in the UK, ranging from a converted pigsty on the Northumberland coast to a Bath House in Warwickshire dating right back to 1748.

National Trust

✆ UK (020) 8315 1111

www.trusty.org

Set in superb, unspoilt locations, the Trust features a range of holiday cottages ranging in size and comfort from a spartan fell cottage in the Lake District to a manor house in Wales.

Quality Cottages

✆ UK (01348) 837874

Specialists in the Welsh coastline and scenic inland mountains, hills and valleys. The very experienced staff visit all 160 properties regularly. Almost all have cots and high chairs. Family discounts apply.

Shamrock Cottages

✆ UK (01823) 660126

shamrock.cottages@binternet.com

Nearly 300 cottages, from simple to luxurious, set in remote and secluded spots in scenic locations across Southern Ireland.

Vere Lodge

✆ UK (01328) 838261

Set in Norfolk, this 8-acre mini-estate of 14 cottages has a toddlers' playground, farm animals, a games room, indoor pool and plenty of sports facilities. A cot, high chair, childgate and babysitting are all on offer. Children are welcomed openly.

Across Europe

Brittany Direct Holidays

✆ UK (020) 8641 6060

Small to medium holiday homes in Brittany, France. All properties provide cots, high chairs and safety gates. Babysitting is available with 48 hours notice.

Catherine Secker

✆ UK (020) 8460 8022

Small family business dedicated to providing first class, tailor-made villa and apartment holidays in northwest Crete.

CV Travel

✆ UK (0870) 603 9018

cv.travel@dial.pipex.com

A range of programmes covering the Greek Islands, Italy, Portugal, France and Spain, with a diverse collection of self-catering properties, including villas with a maid and a cook.

GMF Holidays
☎ UK (01932) 355135
A tailor-made service to the South of France and the Dordogne. Can hire most equipment for children. Babysitters, nannies and childcarers can be arranged.

Interhome
☎ UK (020) 8891 1294
One of the largest selections of privately owned, self-catering homes in Europe.

Laskarina Holidays
☎ UK (01629) 824884
info@laskarina.co.uk
Award-winning operator, specializing in the lesser known Greek islands. Cot hire and linen included in the price for under-2s.

Le Chateau de la Baude
☎ France (490) 289518
Restored, fortified farm in the Vaucluse in Provence. Provides plenty of activities for children. Cots and high chairs are included.

PCI Holidays
☎ UK (01202) 591890
Operators to Spain with on-the-spot English-speaking staff, including babysitters. They have cots and high chairs available for hire and can provide details of local facilities for kids.

Spain at Heart
☎ UK (01373) 836070
spain.at.heart@dial.pipex.com
Elegant properties in rural Andalucia. Staff handle clients as individuals. Welcome hampers provided at most properties. Cots and high chairs available on request

The Best in Italy
☎ Italy (055) 223064
A programme of exceptional ancient and elegant country houses. Cots and high chairs are available. Staff can babysit occasionally.

VFB Holidays
☎ UK (01242) 240340
vfbhol@epinet.co.uk
Character cottages, farmhouses and villas with pools in the loveliest rural and coastal regions of France. Family-friendly operator with generous child discounts.

Villa World
☎ UK (01223) 506554
A villa-only specialist offering high quality properties in Portugal, Spain, the Balearics, Cyprus and the Algarve. Extra beds, cots, high chairs and babysitting can all be arranged.

Worldwide

Barclay International Group
☎ US (212) 832 3777
BarcIntl@ix.netcom.com
Private apartments, villas and cottages available for stays of one night or longer across Europe and the Caribbean.

British Virgin Islands Club
☎ UK (020) 8568 6838
dew@vch.co.uk
Tailor-made holidays to private and secluded villas with pools on the little-known British Virgin Islands.

Condominium Travel Association
☎ US (203) 758 0222
Carefully selected condo rentals available in Europe, the USA, Caribbean, Hawaii, Mexico and Australia.

Home exchange

Hideaways International

✆ US (800) 843 4433 & (603) 430 4433
Thousands of mainly privately-owned properties worldwide, from beachfront villas to central city apartments.

The Individual Traveller

✆ UK (08700) 774774
holidays@indiv-travellers.com
Tailor-made service, featuring carefully selected, quality self-catering properties in the northern states of the USA, Portugal, Spain, Italy and France. Can advise on the most suitable properties for children.

Meon Villas

✆ UK (01730) 268411
www.meontravel.co.uk
Well established operator offering a range of villas across Europe, Florida and St Lucia. Cots automatically arranged for the under-2s. High chairs available on request.

The Villa Agency

✆ UK (01273) 747711
www.thevillaagency.co.uk
Smart holiday villas in the Algarve and in Florida from an operator happy to arrange just about anything required. Cots, high chairs and playpens are available for hire.

My dad never really cared what kind of accommodation he booked so long as it was near a golf course. I remember once we arrived at an absolute flea pit with damp running down the walls and no curtains. My mum was horrified but all my dad said was that it had a great view of the 18th green from the window.

Simon Jones – aged 38

If you need to recharge your batteries but are short of money, then home exchange is one way to do it. Not only is it a cheap option, but it can also provide far more space and amenities than a hotel or B&B. The principle could not be easier. You hand your home over to a family and you take on theirs. The process simply involves you supplying details of your home and family to a company who then list you in their directory, which is circulated to the other members. You can browse through it at your leisure, choosing a country and a property that appeal to you. You then exchange photographs and letters with as many members as you like, before coming to a final decision. References may be checked and a holiday agreement exchanged for added security.

Of course, this arrangement depends on you living in a place that people want to visit and on you having a clean, safe and well-furnished home that meets the agencies' standards.

Once you are satisfied that you meet the criteria, the advantages of home exchange become obvious. You automatically have someone to care for your home, and even your pets, while you are away, offering you guaranteed peace of mind. Most of all, you can afford to visit exotic locations and live in comfortable accommodation (often with the free use of a car) and get to know the area like a true local.

Unlike the accommodation to be found around over-commercialized tourist traps, exchange homes are family homes with none of the impersonal feel of many holiday properties. Most importantly, exchanging homes with a family with children of the same age as yours means their home is certain to be child-proofed and ready supplied with all the baby gear, cots, high chairs, car seats and toys to make your holiday fun and hassle-free. You can exchange ideas with the family of local things to do and places to see. There may even be a local babysitter available.

As for worries about potential damage to your own property and concerns about dishonesty, complaints are rare. Though there is never an absolute assurance, each home exchange is based on mutual respect and trust. Your best security is to get to know your exchange family through corresponding with them in detail. The longer the period of getting to know them, the better the chance of a good rapport. You can always ask a trusted neighbour or friend to check everything is fine.

Bear in mind though that it may take several months or more to find an exchange you are happy with, so you will need to plan well ahead.

Costs

Families of all sizes, including one-parent families, can exchange homes and the savings can be enormous. Your only real expenses are signing up with an agency and transport to your destination. Some companies will undertake all the administration involved in setting up a home exchange, though you are likely to be charged heavily for this service. Of course it does save a lot of time and also removes the element of risk.

If you decide not to take advantage of the agency service, you will still need to establish your own ground rules in a signed agreement. This might cover arrangements for keys, smoking restrictions, fuel usage, telephone calls, and – if a car is involved – vehicle usage and insurance.

Who to contact

Look out for the IHEA (International Home Exchange Association) symbol which incorporates 13 associated agencies worldwide.

In the UK

Home Base Holidays
✆ UK (020) 8886 8752
Established for 13 years, featuring 3,000 properties in around 40 countries. The company is a founder member of the IHEA.

Homelink International
✆ UK (01344) 842642
Over 11,000 properties, mainly in Europe, USA, Canada, Australia, New Zealand and Southern Africa.

**Intervac International
House Exchange Service**
✆ UK (01225) 892208
A long-established company which publishes three directories a year listing 10,000 homes for exchange and rent in more than 40 countries worldwide, as far afield as Madagascar, but mainly in the USA and Europe.

Latitudes House-Swap Register
✆ UK (01273) 581793
Offers a matching service for those who do not want their details published, plus an Internet site. Currently 2,000 properties on their books, worldwide. A member of the IHEA.

Special Families Home Swap Register

✆ UK (01752) 347577

Offer a home exchange service specifically for those with a physical disability.

NCT House-Swap Register

✆ UK (01454) 311426

Has around 200 options in the UK. The register is run partly to raise money for the NCT. Most swappers have children.

Temporary Home Exchange Agency

✆ UK (020) 7482 4010

Features over 3,000 properties throughout Europe, Australia and the USA. A member of the IHEA.

Worldwide Home Exchange Club

✆ UK (020) 7823 9937

An international home exchange directory with some 1,500 listings from 34 countries, including Mexico and the Caribbean.

In the US

At Home Abroad

✆ US (212) 421 9165

Homelink USA

✆ US (800) 638 3841
www.homelink.org

House Exchange Program

✆ US (717) 393 8985

International Home Exchange

✆ US (415) 435 3497

Intervac

✆ US (415) 435 3497
IntervacUS@aol.com

Trading Homes International

✆ US (310) 798 3864

Before you take the plunge

▲ Agree the precise dates that the exchange will take place, together with a cancellation policy.

▲ It helps to come to some agreement over use of fuel and the telephone so you do not get any nasty surprises when you return home and open the bills. It is normal to expect exchange guests to pay for long-distance calls.

▲ Be specific about your requirements, especially about the sort of daily or weekly upkeep you expect, such as feeding the cat, watering the plants, tidying the house, taking telephone messages.

▲ Be clear about your smoking policy.

▲ Pack away anything you would prefer to remain untouched, especially if it is valuable or fragile.

▲ Agree what food, toiletries or other items your visitors can use without having to replace them.

▲ Be clear about what linens and towels can be used.

▲ Consider buying each other bulky items such as nappies, to avoid having to transport them.

▲ Check how your home contents, travel and car insurance is affected if you undertake a home exchange.

▲ Agree to care for your host's home as if it were your own and to leave the house in exactly the same condition as you found it.

Camping

Though camping may mean more work for the adults, it does allow you the freedom to see more of a country than if you were self-catering, and also eliminates having to exhaust yourself trudging around searching for vacant hotel rooms.

If you have never been camping or cara-vanning before – or at least, not since child-hood – it is probably best to head for some-where equipped with luxury caravans, mobile homes or canvas homes ready-erected, ready-equipped and just waiting for you to arrive.

Forget all that pitching your tent each night, wading through mud to start a camp-fire and sharing a bed with mosquitoes. Modern-day, ready-erected campsites bear all the hallmarks of a holiday resort, save the glitzy hotel.

It's not exactly roughing it, as most sites feature tents with separate bedrooms, including integral ground sheets and zip-up doors. There is normally electricity and a full-size fridge. In mobile homes there are even showers and flushable toilets, fitted kitchens and heaters. As for beds, they are no longer inflatables. Some are foam, oth-ers have sprung mattresses. Outdoor seat-ing is often provided too.

Most of these sites give a lot of thought to families and are highly security con-scious, making them ideal for children. The laid-back atmosphere makes for a real break from routine for adults and children alike. In many countries, especially in southern Europe, camping tends to have its own important social agenda, and there are many opportunities to make new friends.

The only real difficulty is relying on the weather, so you are best off choosing a site with plenty of facilities. Many family orien-tated sites offer children's clubs, though the emphasis is usually on entertainment rather than supervised childcare. Bear in mind that on campsites officially qualified chil-dren's representatives are rare and cannot always be depended upon as cover for par-ent's time off. Activity sessions, especially during high season, can be oversubscribed too, and there is often no guarantee that your child will get a place.

What to expect for your money

Campsite ratings and gradings are some-times difficult to assess. These are often based on technical specifications such as pitch size and amenities rather than style and atmosphere so it is probably more important to consider the size of a site. Larger sites generally have more facilities but also more noise and more opportunities for your children to get lost. Unless there are strict restrictions on vehicles, there will also be a good deal more moving traffic.

Traditionally, seaside and forest sites are particularly well geared to children, though as campsites become increasingly sophisti-cated the setting itself is becoming less important in keeping children entertained. At almost all campgrounds nowadays you can expect to find a restaurant or café, a shop for provisions, playground, swimming pool, communal showers, toilets, sinks and a laundry. Some go even further. On Spain's southern coast you will often find bou-tiques, hairdressers, even nightclubs.

It is important to bear in mind one crucial distinction. If you are making a booking from the UK for a mobile home at a campsite, then it is understood that your accommodation will remain stationary. In the USA, on the other hand, a mobile home is expected to be just that. Then your home travels with you as you tour around from campsite to campsite.

Costs

Unless you buy a pre-paid package, assessing costs can become confusing. Sometimes campsites have one set fee, whether it is per tent, per vehicle or per person. More often, your cost will be the sum of several individual charges per child, per adult, per tent and per camper. You will be expected to pay when you arrive. If you are not certain about how long you plan to stay, just pay for the first night and reassess your position the next day.

Having paid, you should keep hold of any receipts or tags that are issued to you, which will prove that you have handed over a sum of money.

Booking

Recommended package operators' campsite programmes to Europe are listed on *page 55*. Of course, you can always turn up at a campsite unannounced and pay as you go. This may be your only option if you are planning on touring. Still, if you already know where you are headed, agencies can also provide a comprehensive booking service worldwide. Try

Eurocamp Independent
✆ UK (01565) 625544

Kampgrounds of America
✆ US (406) 248 7444
www.koakampgrounds.com

Select Site Reservations
✆ UK (01873) 859876

10 reasons to go camping

- Family camping is a good deal cheaper than most self-catering
- It is particularly good value for larger families
- Children have lots of space to themselves and are less likely to feel cooped up
- Camping offers a real, if temporary, change in lifestyle
- There is no timetable to adhere to
- The environment is safe: even the pools are generally supervised
- If you pick a large enough site, there is normally something to suit kids of all ages
- If you are able to drive, you can pack all the children's favourite toys
- Operators often provide flexibility over dates
- Accommodation standards may be higher than in some self-catering properties

Youth hostels

The International Youth Hostel Federation encompasses more than 5,000 hostels in over 70 countries – the largest accommodation network worldwide. Although hostels have always tended to be more readily linked with the college backpack crowds than with family travel, in a bid to attract more grown-ups and families even the youth hostels have shaken off their old house rules and duties, and nowadays can provide a unique, low budget alternative for travelling families.

There are a growing number of youth hostels with family rooms. Some are privately owned but rather more are members of the Youth Hostel Association. The YHA now has over 100 of them in Britain alone, almost 400 in Germany, and at least 100 across the USA.

Despite their draughty, damp old mansion image, the YHA of today boasts modern, family-friendly buildings which can easily cater for smaller parties. Their Family Bunk Rooms are a big draw. These private dormitories come with 4–6 beds, a hand basin and sometimes en suite toilet or shower. Mattresses, pillows and duvets (but not towels) are often provided. Catered meals are usually provided too, though most hostels still have a community kitchen so you can prepare your own meals. You will find that many hostels even offer laundry facilities and a games room.

One thing you are absolutely guaranteed is a communal lounge where you can mix with other guests and use the games, books and toys provided.

For kids, this type of social experience can be a real eye-opener. Characterized by their international flavour, hostels are inevitably places where travellers from around the world gather to swap travel tales and tips, and can provide a real-life lesson in Geography, Sociology and History in a single hit.

Worth bearing in mind

▲ It is hard to define a typical hostel. They can occupy anything from a tin shack to an ancient castle or abbey.

▲ Unless you manage to book a family room, expect dormitory sleeping, usually segregated into his and hers quarters.

▲ Apart from your beds, no other furniture is guaranteed.

▲ You will need to bring your own sheets and towels.

▲ Despite free access to your room throughout the day, most hostels close their doors for part of the day. Access to all other facilities may be for limited hours.

▲ The constant togetherness of hostels allows for little privacy and may lead to some family friction.

Costs

Compared to hotels, family rooms in hostels are very cheap. A family of four can stay overnight in a four-bedded room with en suite facilities at the Liverpool Youth Hostel for example, for as little as £58.30 with breakfast thrown in. Because accommodation in family rooms is often limited, try to reserve a room well before your trip. You may need to persevere. Despite their international bookings network, hostels are still notoriously patchy when it comes to taking bookings.

Booking

All national associations honour reciprocal arrangements, so once you join up, your membership will be acknowledged in any country you visit. Membership often entitles you to discounts at major attractions and on some transport systems worldwide. Be sure to check your handbook for details.

Highland Hostels

℡ UK (01397) 712900
www.highland-hostels.co.uk
These are a group of independently run hostels, mostly set in remote parts of Scotland. Each comes with its own kitchen so you have the freedom to rustle up your own meals as and when you please.

Hostelling International
American Youth Hostels

℡ US (202) 783 6161
dkalter@attmail.com
Family membership costs around $35 per year, and includes all children under 16.

Hostelling International
Membership Services Department

℡ US (800) 444 6111
Become a US member and receive *Hostelling North America*, the official guide to hostels throughout USA and Canada. *Hostelling International: Europe* lists every hostel in 34 European countries.

Youth Hostel Association – Australia

℡ Australia (3) 9670 3802
yha@yhavic.org.au

Youth Hostel Association – UK

℡ UK (01727) 845047 UK
Membership costs £20 for two parents and children under 18, £10 for one parent.

contacts

Rental Directories International

℡ US (215) 985 4001

further reading

Bed and Breakfast: Australia and New Zealand by Jennie Fairlie, Sunstate Press.
Bed and Breakfast in France, published by the AA.
Bed and Breakfast USA by Peggy Ackerman and Betty Rundback, Plume Books.
The Best of the Family Welcome Guide (UK), Poolside Publishing.
Britain's Most Distinctive Bed and Breakfasts by Paul Wade and Kathy Arnold, Duncan Peterson.
The Complete Guide to American Bed and Breakfast by Rik Barnes, Pelican.
Condo Vacations by Pamela Lanier, Lanier.
Families Welcome, published by the English Tourist Board.
The Good Bed and Breakfast Guide, published by Which? Books.
Good Hotel Guide (UK), Ebury.
Home Exchange Vacationing by Bill and Mary Barbour, Rutledge Hill Press.
Irish Bed and Breakfast Book by F. and F. Sullivan, Pelican.
Irish Cottage Holiday Homes Ireland Self-Catering Guide available from Cork Kerry Tourism ℡ Rep of Ireland (21) 273504.
New Zealand Bed and Breakfast Book by J. and J. Thomas, Moonshine Press.
Scotland Bed and Breakfast by Timothy Stilwell, Stilwell Publishing.
Staying off the Beaten Track in England and Wales by Elizabeth and Walter Gundrey, Arrow.

travel as a single parent

Just because you do not have an adult companion, that does not mean you are doomed to spend the rest of your life at home. Just because your partner is too busy to get away, you do not have to follow suit. There are plenty of holiday options that will leave you feeling far from left out. For single parents especially, stress, loneliness and overwhelming responsibilities are all too familiar, even more so when they are struggling to cope on a low income. A break can make all the difference.

Legal matters

Though free package holidays and child discounts vary, often they are only available outside of the school holidays. In the UK parents are legally entitled to take children out of school for up to two weeks for the purpose of a family holiday. (The local education authority may require the parent to fill out a form notifying them of this.)

If you are a lone parent wishing to take a child abroad, but suspect your child's other parent may object, then you should seek legal advice.

When travelling across borders and through immigration to a number of countries (particularly Mexico) single parents are often required to show a letter of permission to travel from the child's other parent. If the other parent is deceased, you will also need proof of this. This may seem to represent bureaucratic excess, but it is not unknown for divorced and estranged spouses to kidnap their own disputed children and smuggle them overseas.

Why it helps to travel

Travelling alone with your children can be a good way to get to know them better. Away from your established home routine, travel can offer you and them the chance to see each other in new and often challenging situations and reinforce the mutual respect so important to your special relationship. You could find you come to depend on each other in a way you will rarely experience at home.

There is no doubt that travel as a single parent is more demanding than if you are part of an adult team. Yet, by demanding a great deal of you, it can help to generate awareness and a heightened sense of your ability not only to survive but to excel at what you already do so well.

Finding a holiday

Many operators, including several cruise lines, cater for both singles and for lone parents. This is ideal if you are planning some well-earned time to yourself.

The advantages of both supervised children's activities and singles' parties are that, while you will want to meet up together for meals and excursions, the rest of the time your children can be kept entertained, and you can enjoy the luxury of picking and choosing your time together. Of course, you do not have to use the children's programmes every day, but they are available when you want some time to yourself.

Though they do not always come cheap, all-inclusive resorts are an especially good choice for lone parent families. Resorts attract a lot of single people as well as single parents, so you won't necessarily be faced with a barrage of cuddling couples. This sort of holiday can offer you the chance to feel like a human being again – not just mum or dad – especially when the children are busy being entertained by the staff. Some resorts even arrange a get-together where singles can meet each other soon after they arrive. Guided adventure trips work too. Many operators arrange trips solely for families, offering offspring instant playmates, while the guides can also give you a break from looking after the children. If your main worry is that you will still feel isolated with nothing in common except for the fact that you are single, then try camping or a villa complex with shared facilities. You will have no problem making friends. For an added sense of security and community, contact the wealth of course centres and 'retreats' worldwide that offer family weeks. While you indulge yourself in all sorts of interests and orientations in relaxing surroundings, your children will be well looked after by like-minded carers.

Holiday share

For some people the thought of holidaying alone with children when everybody else is part of a group may not seem like much fun. One solution is for solo parents to team up with another group or family. Indeed, this may be your only option if you want to manage some types of travel safely (yachting or canal boating, for example).

Taking a holiday with another family will not only cut costs. You will find two heads are better than one when it comes to plan-

Children are not only welcome in a Latin culture – they are seen as a treasure, a reason for celebration. In any Mediterranean bar, there will be a dozen children racing around the tables, being treated to fizzy drink and going about their business under the benevolent eye of the adults.

Elizabeth Luard – *Family Life*

ning your trip, and if you share items you will have far less to pack. Travelling with another family will bring children together and sharing the load with other adults should allow you some time off.

Just be sure to consult with every family member before deciding who to invite. Even the best relationships have been known to crumble over a holiday. You will need to be certain that your interests, disciplining and travelling styles are compatible. It won't work if all you have in common are the children.

On a practical note, it is wise to split all deposit payments as soon as they are due and put verbal agreements (especially concerning refunds and reimbursements should one party cancel) into a friendly note. That way everyone knows where they stand. Make sure all the ground rules are clear, even down to who is supposed to clear up and what time the children need to be in bed by. Try advertising, or get in touch with your local single-parent support group to contact like-minded single parents.

Affording a holiday

From year to year, package holiday operators provide generous reductions for one-parent families. Remember though, that the best value holidays are always snapped up quickly so as a single parent you will need to book as early as possible.

Out of season prices are always much lower than the main holiday periods throughout July and August and during Easter and Christmas time. For younger children not yet caught up in examination timetables, May, early June and early October can be cheaper and far less crowded. At all other times bargains can be found at short notice when unsold holiday packages are heavily discounted.

Whenever you book a package tour, bear in mind that hotel accommodation generally applies to two adults sharing a room. A room accommodating one adult and two or more children can be much harder to find and even more difficult to get a fair price for. You will normally be charged a supplement if you book a single. Look out instead for special family rooms and suites. For self-catering holidays, a larger unit shared between two or more families can work out cheaper, and be more fun.

Group bookings, both for accommodation (particularly out of season) and for many tourist attractions such as theme parks, are often charged at reduced rates. It is always worth enquiring when you book. If you do decide to travel as a group, hiring a minibus can work out less expensive than individual tickets on public transport.

You can save even more money if you search for insurance policies which provide free cover for children under a certain age.

If your finances are stretched, do not rule out a holiday until you have contacted some groups that specialize in holidays for single parents. Local voluntary organizations and charities (including the WRVS, Red Cross and Rotary International) are often involved in arranging and helping with low-cost holidays. To find out if there is any such group in your area, try the public library, your local advice bureau or other local organizations.

Making it work

Compromise is an essential attribute when you are travelling with children, and this applies even more when you are travelling alone with them. If you want the trip to work, then you are going to have to meet your children half way, and vice versa.

One of the hardest things to remember is that the holiday is meant for you as well as your children. It can be difficult to make the break when you feel you do not want to spend a single moment apart from them, especially if they do not live with you full-time. Bear in mind that it will do you both good to spend some leisure time apart. Taking some time to yourself won't mean you are an uncaring parent. Making use of children's programmes, babysitters, clubs and crèches will simply offer you a brief but much-needed rest.

As a parent you too deserve a break from the stresses of everyday life. If you want to enjoy your holiday stay open-minded and receptive to offers of help. You may be surprised by the eagerness of strangers willing to lend a hand. Among many cultures you will discover that children are the responsibility of the entire community, and not just a constant concern for their parents. You will find there are all sorts of people keen to cuddle them and play with your children for a while before reluctantly handing them back. This sort of attitude can be a godsend if you are travelling alone.

Resources

Direct Travel Insurance
✆ UK (01903) 812345
Comprehensive annual travel insurance with
a discount for single parents travelling with
children.

Gingerbread
✆ UK (020) 7336 8183
Information about holidays arranged specifi-
cally for lone parents and their children.

Holidays for One-Parent Families
✆ UK (0161) 370 0337
Arranges UK holidays for lone parents and
their children at discount prices.

National Council for
the Divorced and Separated
✆ UK (0116) 2700595
Promotes over 200 'life-enhancing' courses
both in Greece and the Caribbean.

The Holiday Care Service
✆ UK (01293) 774535
A registered charity which provides support
and information for people whose circumstances make access to holidays difficult.
Free information sheets are available on a
variety of holiday topics.

Holiday Endeavour for Lone Parents
✆ UK (01302) 728791
Charity offering low-cost and subsidized holidays for lone parents and their children,
with major holiday companies throughout
the UK and Spain. Membership is £3 a year.

National Council for
One-Parent Families
✆ UK (020) 7428 5400
Produces a comprehensive booklet full of
helpful advice and ideas. It costs £4.25.

One-Parent Family Holidays
✆ UK (01465) 821288
Specializes in continental holidays for one-
parent families.

Primary Direct Travel Insurance
✆ UK (0870) 444 3434
Offers a discount of 50 percent, charging
half the family rate on a single trip policy.

Travel Companions
✆ UK (01590) 683005
Non-profit making organization that aims to put people who prefer not to travel alone in touch with other like-minded travellers.

Women's Travel Advisory Bureau
✆ UK (01386) 701082
Provides advice, as its name suggests, on issues relating to women travelling on their own or with children.

The Association of Independent Tour Operators (AITO) lists the following members as providing for lone parent families (* indicates members also listed as providing singles holidays).

Anglo Dutch Sports
✆ UK (020) 8289 2808
ads@netcomuk.co.uk
www.netcomuk.co.uk/~ads/html
Established specialists in cycling tours throughout northern Europe.

Argo Holidays*
✆ UK (020) 7331 7063
holidays@argotvl.co.uk
www.argotvl.co.uk/argo
Specialist operator to Cyprus.

Belle France
✆ UK (01797) 223777
✉ (01797) 223666
Walking and cycling holidays.

Classic Collection*
✆ UK (01903) 823088
✉ (01903) 214945
Upmarket holidays to Mallorca, Spain.

Danube Travel*
✆ UK (020) 7493 0263
✉ UK (020) 7224 8959
Breaks, including cruises, to Central Europe.

Esprit Holidays
✆ UK (01252) 616789
www.ski-esprit.co.uk
Alpine family ski and summer sun specialist.

Eurocamp
✆ UK (01565) 626262
enquiries@eurocamp.co.uk
www.eurocamp.co.uk
Ready-erected camping specialists.

Four Seasons
✆ UK (0113) 256 4373
✉ (0113) 255 5923
Self-catering mobile homes and apartments in France.

Keycamp Holidays
✆ UK (020) 8395 4000
Brochure@Keycamp.co.uk
www.keycamp.co.uk
Ready-erected camping specialists.

Okavango Tours and Safaris*
✆ UK (020) 8343 3283
info@okavango.com
www.okavango.com
Tours through southern and central Africa.

Select France
✆ UK (01865) 331350
rheb@globalnet.co.uk
Tailor-made, self-drive holidays to France.

Snowbizz
✆ UK (01778) 341455
www.snowbizz.co.uk
Family ski specialists.

Spanish Harbour Holidays
✆ UK (0117) 986 9777
holidays@spanish-harbour.co.uk
www.spanish-harbour.co.uk
Individually designed family holidays to
northeast Spain.

Travel a la Carte*
✆ UK (01635) 201140
info@travelalacarte.co.uk
www.travelalacarte.co.uk
Self-catering holidays to the Greek Islands.

*Several other established tour operators
also feature special deals for single parents.*

Cosmos
✆ UK (0161) 480 5799
Selected accommodation for one-parent
families.

Roots and Wings Excursions
✆ US (303) 443 7024
Provides a Travel Adventures for Mothers
and Daughters programme.

Shearings
✆ UK (01942) 244246
This coach operator has negotiated double
and twin rooms with no added supplements
at 38 UK hotels.

Skytours
✆ UK (0990) 502552
Special deals for single parents.

Sunworld
✆ UK (01132) 555222
Offer one-parent family savers.

Turkey Specialist
Accommodation Overseas
✆ UK (020) 8977 2984
Recommends, especially for single parent
fathers, its 7-day jeep safari featuring a
series of different activities including fishing,
kayaking and trekking.

Virgin Holidays
✆ UK (01293) 617181
Offer full children's discounts to families with
a single parent at selected hotels in the USA
and in the Mediterranean.

safety

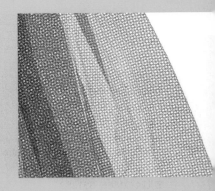

Yesterday Rachel several times begged to be taken to the nearby jungle to monkey-watch, so early this morning we set off, armed with 'rustling sticks' against the local cobras, kraits and vipers, all of which are said to be numerous.

Dervla Murphy – *On a Shoestring to Coorg*

Unfamiliar surroundings, language problems, strange food and drink, even too much sun, can lead to difficulties away from home. But though bad things can inevitably happen, there is little point applying for a passport if you are going to panic over every possible travel emergency. Thankfully, so long as you are careful and stay alert, most problems can normally be avoided. Playing safe on a family trip simply requires intuition, common sense and preparation.

Most holidays inevitably revolve around mealtimes and eating in another country can present a real challenge. Dining hours can be vastly different, menus may be indecipherable and you might not even find any foods you recognize. At the same time you should relish not only having more time to enjoy your food, but the chance to be far more adventurous in what and where you choose to eat.

Facing facts

Children have little real concept of time and asking them to wait for a few weeks for some homestyle food will seem like an eternity. Looking out for the kind of foods they recognize will help make them feel more at ease, even if this turns out to be snacks and packs of processed foods. The fact is your children will not suffer if they do not eat balanced meals every day and they won't end up at the doctor's just because they eat more ice cream than fruit.

Trying new foods

If you know that you are going to have to depend on local food, or you are simply keen for them to give it a try, then give your children an idea of what they are likely to encounter before they arrive. Large supermarkets at home cater for a wide variety of cultural tastes and you can normally find a range of imported foods, including Chinese, Turkish, Mexican, Indian, kosher and all sorts of exotic fruits and vegetables. Try out a few recipes before you travel (but make sure you know how to cook them or your may put your children off for good).

If you are still sure there are going to be problems, you could pack a box of food to take with you containing dry goods such as pasta, cake mixes, packet drinks and snacks. Assorted fun-size boxes of cereal are always a favourite. The amount you can take will depend almost entirely on your mode of transport and how you plan to spend your holiday time once you get there. Unless you plan to spend a good deal of time on foot without a base, this tactic can normally be adopted, but do check about import restrictions at your destination. If these are OK and you are flying, simply check the box through as luggage and collect it at the other end.

Once you arrive, it is probably not worth pressing the food issue too early. Encourage your children by letting them see you try out different foods first. Do not insist that they follow suit. Try to order a selection of more familiar dishes along with unusual ones. You can always resort to bribing your children with a local coin or dessert for each new one they try. Keep it fun. At least you will have made the effort.

Eating out

A family trip is probably not the best time to try out the swanky new restaurant everyone has been telling you about. If you must hit a gourmet spot, then call first to check whether children are welcome. Ask whether they have high chairs and children's items on the menu. If they do, it is probably a good sign. Try to eat early. If the restaurant accepts reservations, telephone well ahead of time, even if you are planning an early dinner. There may be several other families trying the same tactic. To cut down on waiting time, ask whether you can make your order in advance over the telephone.

If the restaurant does not accept reservations, be sure to arrive before peak hours to avoid long queues for a table. Avoid an empty restaurant. Unless you know the locals dine late (as in Spain and Italy) there is usually a very good reason why nobody eats there. Check the menu outside the door first to make sure there is at least one thing you will each be willing to eat. Carry quiet toys, books, crayons and a pad of paper to keep your children busy. A portable booster seat, fabric 'handbag high chair' or seat that bolts to the table is always worth carrying for impromptu meals with toddlers. If you are eating later than you anticipated, you can always have your children dressed in their pyjamas so that later on getting them to bed will be that much easier.

A hungry or restless child won't wait patiently. Ask for some bread to be brought to the table so that your child can get started straight away. Make it clear that your children's meals can be served first, but ask that the food should not be too hot to touch. If, despite your efforts, your child throws a tantrum or becomes difficult, then a trip to the bathroom or a walk outside should restore some calm.

For better or worse, fast-food chains are just about everywhere these days. They often have playgrounds and picnic tables, as well as clean and spacious toilets. Familiar enough to be comfortable, yet different enough to be interesting, fast-food chains in foreign places are just about guaranteed to keep your children smiling.

Eating in

Surrender to your children's needs. The gourmet experience is fine once in a while but daily dining out is rarely a child's idea of heaven. There will be plenty of occasions when you will find your children wholly unreceptive to sitting quietly at a table for an hour. Children love room service. Ordering out, then eating in your room in front of the TV might be a one-off treat or – more likely – just what they are used to back home. Either way it is a perfect chance for you to relax. If you have two separate rooms, let them eat in one while you take some time out in the other. If they are old enough to stay in the room by themselves for a while, you could even pop downstairs for an adults-only dinner. Room service menus almost always feature favourites such as pizza, pasta, sandwiches and burgers. If it all looks too pricey, then order in a pizza, or bring back a takeaway. Most hotels have no objection and the savings can be considerable.

Food on the go

Full-blown meals are not always accessible when your children get hungry. Always carry some nutritious, non-crushable snacks with you, such as dried fruit bars, nuts, muesli bars, raisins or raw carrot sticks. If you are out for the day, these snacks may be in your bag for quite some time. Avoid anything that could leak, crumble or turn to mush.

If you are planning a long trip, then children are likely to be confined to a small space for long periods. Avoid snacks that are high in sugar, chocolate and caffeine. A hyped-up toddler with nowhere to go is no fun at all.

Picnicking en route gives the children something to look forward to and allows them some space to let off steam. Pack a tempting lunch, but do not fuss with kitchenware from home. Disposable plates, bowls and cutlery are far more practical.

Self-catering

Guidebooks rarely offer advice on how to shop for basics when you are away. Though you may want to bring a few favourites from home, anybody renting accommodation is certain to need more supplies, usually on a daily basis.

One of the first things you will need to do is find out when the food shops are open. Some close at the weekends. Others close early, or even for long gaps in the mid-afternoon. Public holidays especially can catch you off guard.

Though it is hard to imagine, you will normally find more shops per community in less developed countries than you will find at home. Supermarkets are generally small and compact and four or five shops selling similar products are often grouped together intentionally. What you will actually find in each shop might be anyone's guess. Though the basics such as meat, eggs, bread, flour, oats, cheese, rice and coffee are almost universal, you cannot always expect a huge selection. Instead of six types of pasta, you may just find one. Convenience foods are often few and far between and are frequently of poor quality. Unsweetened fruit juice can be impossible to find.

Even with a modest shopping list, it might take several visits to several stores before your shopping basket is near full. Even then, you should not depend on a critical item being available every day. When stock runs out, deliveries can be unpredictable. It is often worth remembering to buy today what you know you will need tomorrow.

In the absence of anything familiar, baked potatoes, boiled eggs, nuts and live yoghurt are a safe bet.

More dependable and always enticing, street vendors and open air markets thrive worldwide. Small places often have market day just once a week; larger ones may have a daily market. If so, you will normally find it under cover near the town centre. Here local farmers sell their freshest produce at the lowest prices. You can normally find anything you need. Better still, the quality of the produce, fruit, vegetables, meat, cheese, baked goods, grains, dried fruit, eggs, spices and nuts, is likely to be better than your supermarket back home.

Certainly it will be fresher. Browse around the market and patronise stalls that seem popular with the locals. Choose your own produce and do not be bullied into letting the stallholder pick it for you. If the vendor refuses, move on.

Be careful to observe the shopping etiquette of those in the know. In some places, patient queuing is expected. In others, queuing will get you nowhere and you will need to push and shove your way to the front of a crowd.

If your biggest hurdle is likely to be bridging the language gap, then tourist areas are usually the easiest to shop in, because shopkeepers will often speak English. A novel way to convey your needs if you really can't find the word in a guide or dictionary is to use a wordless phrase book, which allows you merely to point at a picture of what you want.

Staying healthy

Whenever possible drink water, and plenty of it, to help avoid the obvious inconveniences of constipation. It also helps to eat some form of fresh, well peeled fruit or vegetable every day.

You can help avoid upset tummies on the first few days of your arrival by cutting out especially rich and spicy foods. All children are prone to bouts of diarrhoea and vomiting, of course, and these are not always connected to what they have eaten. Unfortunately, though, most diarrhoea is a result of unhygienic food preparation, mainly from unclean hands.

If there is one thing you can do to avoid getting sick on holiday, it is to try to be

meticulous about hygiene. Wash your own hands before touching food or feeding your children, and try to make sure they wash their hands properly too. This is especially important if you have been petting animals. If this is a real problem, briskly rubbing your hands together will be some help in getting rid of potentially harmful bacteria.

Generally, hot freshly cooked dishes are undoubtedly the safest foods. Beware of reheated foods, which must be cooked very thoroughly. Even the plainest dish (such as fried rice) may be made from barely reheated left-overs and can be a paradise for all manner of germs.

Cold cooked food can be just as risky. Unless you know how long your pizza, quiche or other tempting buffet snack has been hanging around without proper refrigeration, then it is probably best avoided. Flies fussing around the food only add to the risks.

Seafood can carry hepatitis. If you are not certain that it is fresh and clean, then only eat it once it has been thoroughly cooked and served to you piping hot. If you have doubts, then at all costs avoid eating raw seafood. It may carry cholera.

In some places you may need to think twice before offering your children ice cream and other dairy products, including custards, non-live yoghurt, cream fillings and mayonnaise. In Africa, India and parts of the Middle East, in particular, you cannot always be sure that milk has been pasteurized or that dairy products have been properly refrigerated. Unpasteurized cheeses and milk products are common in many parts of Europe, especially France. Double-check sell-by dates and weigh up the general cleanliness of the shop to get some idea of how fresh the produce is likely to be. If in doubt, you should opt for long-life, powdered or tinned milks.

In many developing countries, crops may be irrigated using untreated sewage or even fertilized with untreated human waste. Here fruit and vegetables that grow closest to the soil are particularly dangerous. Strawberries and lettuce are two of the worst affected. Contrary to certain product assurances, soaking these high-risk foods in chemicals such as iodine will not render them harm-free. The best all-round maxim to adopt in poorer countries is *peel it, boil it, cook it, shell it or forget it*. If you are keen on salad, stick to carefully washed and peeled cucumber, and the less susceptible shiny-skinned fruit and vegetables (such as tomatoes), so long as they are not punctured or scarred. Lettuce should be resolutely avoided in countries where hepatitis, typhoid or other bacterial infections are a distinct possibility.

Finally, assuming that you are selective about where you eat and what you eat, bear in mind that streetside snack bars and market cafés often have such a rapid turnover of local customers that their food rarely has a chance to go bad and could easily turn out to be safer than some international cuisine cooked in 5-star hotels.

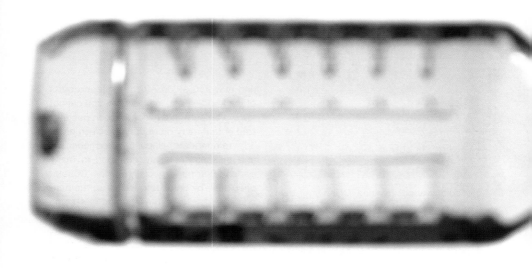

contacts

The AnywayUp Cup
✆ UK (029) 2057 5600

BW Technologies
✆ UK (0990) 820 000
For details of their newly-developed water filter system.

Childcare Products
✆ UK (0161) 427 8598
Produce a travel bottle warmer.

Cotswold
✆ UK (01285) 860612
Their shops sell a range of water purification devices.

Pur
✆ UK (01438) 748884
For their Voyager water purifier.

further reading

The Wordless Travel Book by Jonathon Meader, Ten Speed Press.

Drinks

Travelling can leave you feeling dehydrated. Be sure to take along a water bottle filled with a favourite drink – preferably diluted, as juices and artificially sweetened drinks tend to increase thirst rather than quench it. You can buy bottles of ready mixed baby juice which not only save trouble (whatever age your children) but are also sugarless, with no preservatives. Boxed drinks with straws keep most children happy, though these are notoriously easy to squeeze, squirt and spill. You can buy special, non-squeezable plastic holders for them. Otherwise, a drinking cup with a non-spill lid is a safe bet. The AnywayUp Cup is a favourite. Older children are likely to con-sider a squeezy sports bottle top much more credible.

It is reassuring to know that foreign water is nowhere near as hazardous as travellers are usually led to believe. At the same time

it is always worth taking some basic precautions. In Morocco, for instance, the tap water in northern cities is considered safe to drink, while elsewhere in the country it is not. Boiled tap water is by far the safest option. Carrying a thermos filled with boiled water allows for all sorts of eventualities.

Chemical sterilization is the most convenient, if least effective, method of improving water quality. Iodine tablets or crystals will produce drinkable water within 20 minutes. A simple new water filter system, Pur Voyager, approved by the International Survivors Instructors Association, is said to produce water as safe as if it were boiled. It is easy to set up, robust and delivers a litre of drinking water each minute. This type of equipment can normally be found at camping outlets.

When it comes to buying drinks overseas, stick to those you know to be safe. If you notice local people drinking out of plastic bottles, the chances are the tap water is unsafe to drink. Unfortunately, there is no absolute guarantee that even shop-bought bottled water is safe. It may simply be treated tap water. It may also contain unsuitable mineral levels for younger children. Always check that bottle seals are intact before you indulge, and in restaurants try to insist that bottles are opened at your table, within view. It is worth remembering that most brand-name carbonated drinks, such as Coca-Cola and Pepsi, are bottled under strict sanitary conditions worldwide.

Cutting costs

In lots of places you will find local eating stalls and restaurants that are safe, appetizing and cheap. Realistically, though, there will be times when all your children will settle for is a fancy restaurant or hotel. It might be because other eateries look unsavoury, or simply because their menus do not appeal to your children. Either way, an occasional indulgence is sure to be worth the pleasure it brings. Big hotels just about anywhere in the world can serve up the fast-food standard of a burger, shake and fries. Try not to let your children win you over every time. Agree to limit the treats and let them know that by saving on meals you will have extra money to spend on them elsewhere on the holiday.

If you want to take a break from cooking, but do not want to have to spend a fortune on food, choose an all-inclusive resort that covers breakfast, lunch, dinner, drinks and snacks in the base price.

If you just want to keep an eye on your food expenses, then most holiday packages can include a meal option (look out for bed and breakfast or full board).

If you plan to save money and also keep some control over your family's diet, bring along a well stocked cooler box. Hotel mini-bars are a particularly expensive haven for hungry youngsters. Empty the contents into your bag or box, then replace the costly items with your own shop-bought snacks. Just be sure to notify the staff that you will be returning their untouched booty when you leave.

Feeding your baby

Babies are easy to please on long trips. If you are considering weaning your baby, put it off until after your trip. as continuity will help smooth your passage. What is more, since milk is all babies need for the first six to eight months, their travel needs are naturally simplified. Breastfeeding removes the need for bulky bottles and bags. Global attitudes still differ towards nursing but a little diplomacy with a well-manœuvred cardigan or blanket is usually enough to alleviate tensions.

If your baby is bottle-fed, invest in some ready mixed cartons that do not need to be refrigerated. Take along plenty of sterilized water, extra pre-measured sachets of powdered formula, a thermos and a bottle sterilizer. Some bottle warmers plug directly into a car cigarette lighter. Another ingenious model made by Childcare consists of an insulated sleeve that just needs a squeeze to make the crystals inside it react and start to heat up. If you can, get your baby used to room-temperature or even cold milk. It will save you a lot of time and trouble when you are on the move.

Any baby will tell you (given half a chance) that the formula they are used to is best and anything else tastes just awful. You will be able to buy powdered baby milk almost everywhere overseas, but brands may not be familiar and, even if they are, the formulas will not necessarily be the same. It is far better to take your own. If you do happen to run out, take the empty tin to the local pharmacy and ask them for the nearest similar brand. If you shop locally, be certain that you buy only milk formulated

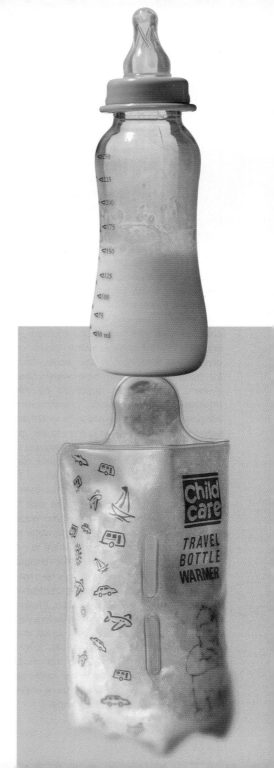

especially for a baby, and not just dry milk, which will be unsuitable.

Babies almost everywhere in the world are fed out of jars and packets, and your baby will not go hungry. Boxes of instant baby cereal are widely available. Pre-mixed with powdered formula, or dry milk, and ready measured into a sealable travel bowl, you need only add warm water for an instant meal.

If you are venturing off the tourist track, check on availability first with embassies or tourist boards. The only real difficulty you are likely to encounter is that you may not recognize familiar brands and ranges of baby food. Even if you can they may be made to a different formula and will not necessarily taste the same. For example, Milupa, a German company, sell extensively in Europe. The packets you find abroad, however, may not be familiar ones. Not only do different governments have different rules about what goes into baby foods, but foreign babies often have different tastes.

If you are looking for Milupa products you will often find them in pharmacies rather than supermarkets. One familiar brand of baby food you might find overseas is Heinz; Gerber and Nestlé are both readily available as well.

Always check contents for additives. Some countries are stricter than others about what they feed their babies. Watch out for added sugar and salt. Also check on whether cereals are added, as you may not want to feed a young baby wheat. Gluten-free and organic products are becoming increasingly available.

One of the problems with introducing babies to new foods while you are away is that they may get addicted to them and start rejecting their old foods once they return home. Try to take a few favourites from home. The smaller jars of baby food fit neatly, and will stay at the right temperature, inside a wide mouth thermos. Do not take unopened tins in your hold luggage on a plane, though, as they may explode under the unpressurized conditions. A battery-operated food grinder will allow your baby to share preferred foods from your plate wherever you happen to be eating.

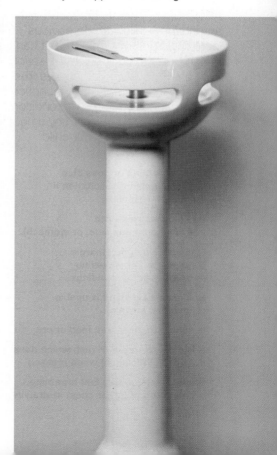

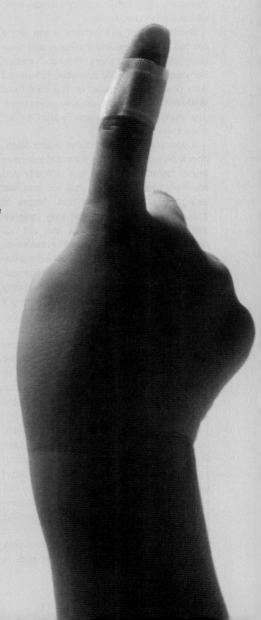

medical matters

Danger signs requiring urgent action

All too often, parents are faced with an unhappy child with no obvious localizing signs or symptoms. It can be hellish trying to distinguish the serious from the relatively trivial. Always trust your intuition, especially if you notice a deterioration in your child's condition. Seek a doctor urgently, at any time of the day or night, if your child

- Stops breathing or goes blue (lift child; begin resuscitation if there is no response).

- Has a convulsion or fit (roll child onto one side, or stomach).

- Is unconscious or lethargic, disorientated or shows no awareness of surroundings.

- Has glazed eyes and is unable to focus on anything.

- Is unable to drink, eat, feed or cry.

- Has a purple-red skin rash which does not go white (blanch) when pressed.

- Shows signs of very fast breathing, grunting breathing or chest in-drawing.

Finding a doctor

If the need arises, the best place to enquire about medical facilities is the local tourist bureau or any large hotel. In a capital city embassies will have lists of the most reliable clinicians. They will recommend doctors who speak English and direct you to reliable services and pharmacies. Facilities can vary dramatically, but even in a less developed area where the hospitals seem positively archaic, there will often be private practices available with a much higher level of medical expertise. Of course you will need to prove you are capable of paying for any private medical care before the doctor can help you.

Visiting a doctor, hospital or pharmacy abroad can be daunting. Do not be put off by first appearances. Just because the equipment may look antiquated or unfamiliar does not mean the doctor does not know his profession. Many doctors worldwide will have completed some part of their training in European or American medical schools. If communication does proves difficult, ask whether they have a medical language dictionary available. This will usually give medical terms both in English and in the local language.

No matter where you want to go on holiday, worrying about your children's health and what type of medical services might be available should never keep you from travelling. While the list of potential problems may seem off-putting, there are a range of medical services worldwide that can provide emergency assistance and advice whenever it is needed. Some useful numbers include

SOS Assistance SA
✆ Switzerland (22) 347 6161
The team promises to deliver blood by courier to anywhere in the world.

HotelDocs
✆ US (800) 468 3537
Provides doctors in 150 US cities. A doctor can usually get to your hotel within 35 minutes.

International Association for Medical Assistance to Travellers (IAMAT)
✆ US (716) 754 4883
✆ Canada (519) 836 0102
IAMAT is a non-profit foundation. Membership entitles you to a worldwide directory of English-speaking physicians, hospital locations and fixed prices on medical services. IAMAT also provide climate, malaria, sanitation and immunization advice.

A medical directory

One of the most worrying aspect of travelling overseas is the thought of your children suddenly falling ill. Far from home, the sight of a young one knocked out by dysentery or a tropical disease the name of which you cannot even pronounce may be more than you can stand and bring your holiday to an untimely and worrying end. However, things need not always be so serious and keeping your family healthy is basically a matter of two equally important strategies: first, taking sensible preventive measures; and second, knowing what to do in case of a sudden illness.

Many holiday disasters can be avoided in the first place if you pay special attention to hygiene and obey some basic, common-sense rules. A little medical knowledge and some well chosen supplies can go a long way towards keeping any illness from interfering with your holiday plans. Almost all of the natural remedies listed here can be safely used in conjunction with conventional prescription medications. Though they can help relieve symptoms considerably, it is not recommended that they be used on their own as a cure. *The World Traveller's Manual of Homeopathy* by Dr Colin Lessell can tell you more. Although we have attempted to offer advice on the appropriate age for specific medications, it is still always best to check with your doctor or the instructions provided by the manufacturer.

Air pressure

When you fly, bring a children's pain reliever and decongestant. If you know your child suffers from ear pain during flights, ask your doctor or pharmacist for advice on giving a dose of decongestant (such as ephedrine, suitable for children over three months as a single dose) during travel as a preventative measure. Breastfeeding or offering a bottle to infants during both take-off and landing can help to relieve ear pressure. Older children can try chewing gum, sucking a sweet or continuous swallowing. In addition, there are products available (such as disposable ear-plugs) that will help reduce flight-related discomfort. Look out for Earplane ear-plugs.

Allergy

A useful over-the-counter remedy for a range of mild allergies is Piriton, which is suitable for all children over 12 months. Any member of your family who has a history of suffering severe allergic reactions should travel with everything they might need in case of an emergency, as well as appropriate identification. Medical identity bracelets are available from

Medic-Alert Foundation
✆ UK (020) 7833 3034

Medic-Alert Foundation
✆ US (209) 668 3333

Natural remedies

❀ Honey and apple cider in a glass of warm water is claimed to help prevent allergies.

❀ Eat the local honey or try nettle tea if you suffer from hay fever.

❀ Lavender essential oil, in a light carrier oil, can be massaged into the affected area or the chest to reduce spasm and generally boost immunity.

❀ Evening primrose oil can help prevent allergies in susceptible people.

❀ Take steps to boost immunity by increasing intake of magnesium, A, B and C vitamins, and iron (within the recommended doses).

Altitude sickness

High altitude affects some individuals more than others and can even be fatal. Symptoms include headaches, dizziness, insomnia, a dry cough and nausea. Though children acclimatize faster than adults, they are more susceptible and tend to succumb more quickly. It can be especially difficult to diagnose warning symptoms in children under the age of two. If altitude sickness is suspected, the first course of action is to suspend or limit all activity for a day or two. Next, drink as much water as you possibly can. The air is thinner at high altitudes, so you breathe more frequently and thus lose more water as you exhale. Children do not usually drink unless they are thirsty, so you will have to keep track to ensure they consume at least 6–8 glasses each day. Mild altitude problems will generally abate within 48 hours. It is important to ascend slowly and take frequent rest days from then on. If symptoms persist, the only treatment is to descend. Watch out for increasing fatigue and disorientation as these are danger signs and may require medical attention.

Antibiotics

The use of antibiotics is increasingly controversial, due to their overuse and potential ineffectiveness as more and more infections build up a resistance to them.

If you or your children are prescribed oral antibiotics abroad, make sure that they are completely necessary. If they are, be sure to complete the full course. The most useful broad-spectrum antibiotic for children is amoxycillin. If your child is allergic to penicillin, be sure that the doctor you consult understands this. If there is a serious reaction to any antibiotic you use, stop taking it immediately. Tetracycline antibiotics should never be taken by children or during pregnancy.

Natural remedies

🌼 Peel and thoroughly chew one quarter of one sweet white onion, raw or cooked, 2–4 times a day.

🌼 Peel and chew three cloves of garlic, 2–4 times a day.

🌼 Watercress contains benzyl mustard oil, which is a powerful antibiotic.

🌼 Barberry is a proven antibiotic. It is an extremely powerful herb and should only be used in small doses under supervision. Avoid during pregnancy.

🌼 Live yoghurt (or acidophillus supplements) can be taken to increase beneficial bacteria in the gut following a course of antibiotics. Probiotics International make suitable children's supplements.

Antihistamines

Antihistamines are used to relieve symptoms of mild allergy and itching from widespread insect bites or stings. Antihistamine creams and ointments should be avoided as sensitivity to them can occur following exposure to strong sunlight. Oral medications are preferable, either in syrup or tablet form. Piriton and Clarityn are suitable for children over 12 months, though both tend to cause drowsiness. Phenergan is often prescribed solely for its soporific effect – as a mild sedative for small children and occasionally for fractious children on long and tedious journeys. If you are considering using an antihistamine for this purpose, you will need to be aware that some children react adversely, becoming cranky and overactive if the dose is not right.

Aspirin

Some foreign medications may contain aspirin, which your children would not be given at home.

Bilharzia

Bilharzia is a potentially troublesome parasite which spends its early life in freshwater snails then swims free in search of fresh skin to inhabit. It is common in freshwater rivers, streams, lakes and dams in much of Africa, the Middle East, Brazil, Venezuela and some Caribbean islands. In any of these areas it is altogether unsafe to swim.

It is also possible to acquire bilharzia from bathing in contaminated water in problem areas. It is best to ask locally for advice. It is important to towel dry vigorously in all suspect areas.

Once the minute worms enter the skin, they infect the intestines or bladder where they start to produce large numbers of eggs. A high fever can result, eventually culminating in blood-stained urine and intense abdominal pain. Symptoms can take up to six weeks to develop, but sometimes people may not show any symptoms at all until it is too late. The parasite may cause severe neurological damage. Recommended drug treatments include niridazole and praziquantel.

Choking

If a child chokes, collapses and goes blue, it is most likely that an object, toy or a piece of food has been inhaled. First check the mouth and, if the object is easily removable, take it out. If nothing can be seen, place the child with their abdomen facing your knee (head downwards) and try five sharp blows on the back, between the shoulder blades, which may help dislodge the object. If unsuccessful, turn the child face up and apply pressure to the lower part of the ribcage at short intervals. Repeat. If there is no response, turn the child back onto its abdomen and repeat five sharp blows to the back. A baby should be held upside down and slapped on the back five times. If this does not work you will also need to apply pressure to force the object out. An unconscious child should be laid down face up. Sit astride the hips and place a hand on the abdomen (between the belly button and ribcage). Thrust downwards 3–4 times at an angle towards the child's head. Applying force to the bottom of the ribcage can also prove successful.

Lay a baby face up on your lap with the head on your knees. Place the tips of two fingers side by side on each hand on the lower ribcage. Press firmly but gently upwards 4–5 times. Abdominal thrusts are not recommended for babies because of the potential risk to internal organs.

Cholera

Cholera is characterized by a sudden onset of acute diarrhoea, vomiting, muscular cramps and fatigue. Fluid loss is the main worry, and treatment for dehydration is the most important aspect of treatment alongside an antibiotic such as ampicillin. Medical help should be sought immediately if you suspect cholera. Because the bacteria responsible for this disease are waterborne, paying close attention to food hygiene should help protect travellers. There is currently no vaccine for cholera.

Constipation

This is a surprisingly common complaint. All sorts of factors can contribute to the problem, including jetlag, changes in diet, dehydration, even a reluctance to use unfamiliar toilets. A high intake of fluids and a high fibre diet are preferable to medication (dried fruit, whole grains, dried beans, nuts, peeled fruit and vegetables are best). If all else fails a gentle sugar-based preparation such as Lactulose should help. Docusole 100 is suitable for children from six months and is also available without prescription.

Natural remedies

✿ Gentle laxative herbs include licorice, marshmallow root, buck thorn and senna leaves, which should be taken as a herbal infusion. Rhubarb root can also be drunk as an infusion.

✿ Massage a few drops of marjoram, rosemary or fennel oil, diluted in grapeseed oil, into the abdomen for relief.

✿ Acidophilus supplements will encourage the health of the intestines and make bowel movements more regular.

Creeping eruption

Children on holiday spend a good deal of time without their shoes on. If you are travelling to Sri Lanka, Thailand, West Africa, Florida or the Caribbean, in particular, your children may pick up hookworm larvae from dog or cat mess when they walk barefoot on the beach. The parasite is pretty harmless, but wanders aimlessly under the skin, causing itching and sometimes blistering, usually on the feet. If you suspect creeping eruption, consult a doctor. Treatment is effective using Mintezol or ethyl chloride which works to cool the skin. Both remedies also kill the larvae.

Cuts and grazes

These can easily become infected in hot climates and may be difficult to heal. Coral cuts, for example, are notoriously slow to heal, as coral injects venom into a wound.

Clean any wound as soon as you can with plenty of soap and water, removing as much dirt and gravel as possible. Next apply a mild antiseptic cream or lotion. A dry powder spray (such as Savlon Dry) does not sting. Cover with a sticky plaster until bedtime, when allowing the clean air to get to it will help it heal more quickly.

For any cut beyond the plaster stage, or for any that become infected, allow it to bleed to ensure cleanliness, wash scrupulously with boiled water, then bandage with gauze. Applying aloe vera gel first can aid healing. Stitches are best avoided if at all possible. Steristrips and butterfly closures are better alternatives.

Natural remedies

- A few drops of tea tree oil, in warm water, can be used to clean a wound and act as an antiseptic.

- Geranium oil can be dropped onto a dressing to encourage healing.

- Lemon juice is an excellent styptic. Once diluted, it can be applied directly to a clean wound. A tiny pinch of cayenne pepper, applied direct, will also help stop bleeding.

- Use a witch hazel compress on wounds and swellings.

- Homeopathic treatment includes arnica to limit bruising and encourage healing, plus calendula or hypericum tinctures to clean the wound.

Dehydration

It is easy to get dehydrated in hot temperatures and during long flights. It can occur especially rapidly in small children, causing fatigue, dizziness and headaches. Encourage your children to drink plenty of water. They should be drinking enough to ensure their urine is consistently pale and unclouded. If children do become dehydrated, use oral rehydration solutions (such as Dioralyte) to help them recover quickly. If your child becomes listless and unresponsive try pinching a fold of skin on the stomach. When released the skin should spring back to its normal smooth surface. If it does not, seek urgent medical attention.

Diarrhoea

The most common holiday complaint is diarrhoea. Two-fifths of all international travellers suffer from it. While it is inconvenient at best, diarrhoea can be serious in very young children, especially when it leads to dehydration. Thankfully, the course of diarrhoea is normally short-lived and self-limiting. More importantly, though, by easing yourself into new foods gradually and taking simple precautions, it can often be avoided altogether.

Prevention

Most travellers' diarrhoea is caused by micro-organisms that enter the body through contaminated food and drink. These may be on your hands or on the food itself. To avoid diarrhoea (and a number of other miserable diseases including dysentery, giardiasis, hepatitis A, typhoid and polio) your family should stick to the following hygiene principles.

▲ Always wash your hands whenever you eat and whenever you feed your children.

▲ Use only purified water and ice, or carbonated drinks you know to be safe.

▲ Brush teeth using safe water and do not let your children swallow the bath water.

▲ Only eat piping hot food that comes to your table literally steaming. Send back anything that is lukewarm or that you suspect may have been lying around, especially shellfish and seafood.

▲ Only consume pasteurized milk and dairy products. Long life and powdered milks are safe to use.

▲ Avoid buffet snacks in warm countries, especially cold cut meats. Bacteria multiply fast under such conditions and flies may settle on the food without you noticing.

▲ Ensure you wash and peel fruit and vegetables.

▲ Avoid intricately prepared meals that require a lot of handling or ingredients that may need to be pre-cooked and reheated.

Cure

For children under the age of 12 months, diarrhoea can be critical. The most important aspect of treatment is replacing lost fluids and salts. The best way of doing this is to drink a special preparation such as Dioralyte. If this is not readily available, then a drink containing both salt and sugar is useful. Weak black tea with sugar, or carbonated drinks allowed to go flat with a pinch of salt, will both help. Pharmacies should also be able to provide you with ready mixed sachets which simply need to be added to drinking water. Even a child who is vomiting should be able to absorb the solution by taking small sips frequently. Ease back into a normal diet with plain foods such as bananas, toast, potatoes and rice. Avoid any fried or raw foods (other than bananas).

Diocalm is a useful symptomatic remedy for adults and children over six, and is available without a prescription. For settling the stomach, kaolin-based Pepto-Bismol and Milk of Magnesia are safe medications for children over the age of six. Avoid codeine, or any drug which acts to paralyse the bowel.

Most cases of diarrhoea clear up within three days. If your child has five or more watery bowel movements a day for three or more consecutive days, seek medical advice. If diarrhoea is accompanied by fever or blood loss, consult a doctor as soon as possible. Only accept antibiotics if a serious infection, such as salmonella, is suspected as, prescribed inappropriately, antibiotics can make matters even worse.

Natural remedies

- Fresh lemon juice with warm water will help fight infection and cleanse the system.

- Add plenty of honey to warm water and sip for its antibacterial and immune-enhancing properties.

- Licorice tea will help to flush out the toxins.

- Rub a little diluted lavender oil into the abdomen to reduce spasms.

- Carrot juice is useful for children's diarrhoea.

Dysentery

Dysentery is caused by contaminated food or water. Its symptoms are severe diarrhoea (often with blood or mucus) or a fever, or sometimes both. There are two types of dysentery and one (amoebic) is often more gradual in its onset. Any signs of dysentery require prompt and skilled medical attention. Antibiotic treatment and rehydration should improve the symptoms.

Natural remedies

✿ Onion juice has been used to help treat amoebic dysentery.

Earache

Ear infections are caused by congestion in the ear and are more frequent on holiday, usually due to more frequent swimming. Ears are best towel-dried thoroughly after a swim. Antibiotic treatment with amoxycillin is usually necessary if the earache is intense and prolonged or accompanied by fever. Swimming must be avoided until recovery is complete. Though it is not ideal, it is not normally necessary to postpone flying if you have an ear infection.

Natural remedies

✿ Homeopathic treatments include belladonna for pain and redness, aconite for sudden attacks of sharp pain and pulsatilla when there is a feeling of pressure behind the eardrum.

Fever

A temperature of 39°C or above should be regarded as a fever. Children often have fevers for little apparent reason and recover from them within a few hours. Most of the causes of a fever overseas are likely to be the same as they are at home (colds, respiratory infections, tonsillitis). The general rule for treating fever is to cool children down as quickly as possible, administer some paracetamol and let them sleep. However, when there are signs of fever and you are travelling within a malaria belt, the possibility of malaria should always be a serious consideration. Fever with diarrhoea may indicate dysentery. Fever with any combination of neck stiffness,

First-aid kit

headache, a blotchy rash and an inability to tolerate bright lights can be the signs of meningitis. Areas with recurring meningitis epidemics are Mongolia, Vietnam, Brazil, the Sahara, the Nile Valley and rural Nepal. A doctor should be alerted to these sort of symptoms immediately.

Natural remedies

❁ Both linden and yarrow tea are excellent for all feverish conditions.

❁ Black pepper and pyrogen can both be used as homeopathic remedies to help lower body temperature.

❁ Lime and lemongrass have fever-reducing properties and are commonly used in aromatherapy.

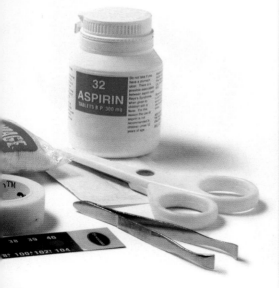

Always carry a first-aid kit with essentials customized for your destination, and remember that it is not always easy to find children's drugs when you are travelling. For a wide selection of concise baby and toddler first-aid guides try the St John's Ambulance.

▲ antihistamine (for bites, allergies, colds, even motion sickness)

▲ antiseptic cream and wipes and dry antibiotic powder

▲ appropriate antimalarial medications (as prescribed)

▲ calamine lotion and aloe vera gel (for soothing burns, bites and stings)

▲ decongestant

▲ diarrhoea remedy and oral rehydration sachets such as Dioralyte

▲ insect repellents

▲ paracetamol or analgesic preparation

▲ pre-sterilized, disposable syringe and needle

▲ protective lip balm

▲ scissors and tweezers (for removing ticks and splinters)

▲ sticky plasters, sterile wound dressings and bandages

▲ tea tree oil and lavender oil

▲ thermometers (take a strip thermometer, mercury ones are banned on planes)

▲ travel sickness preparations

▲ water purification supplies

▲ zinc-based sun creams

Giardiasis

This intestinal disorder is caused by a par-asite present in contaminated water. Symptoms include a bloated stomach, cramps, vomiting, gas and diarrhoea. These symptoms may come and go, and continue for several weeks following exposure to the parasite. Tinidazole or metronidazole preparations normally bring rapid relief.

Heatstroke

Heatstroke is caused by an acute loss of water and salt deficiency following expo-sure to high temperatures. It results in fail-ure of the body's heat control mechanisms and is a form of shock. This can be espe-cially dangerous in children, causing nau-sea, throbbing headaches, a high tempera-ture, disorientation and dehydration. In mild cases, it is often possible simply to increase fluid intake, and replace lost salts by using salt more liberally during mealtimes or by using salt tablets. In severe cases, however, delirium and physical collapse can eventu-ally occur. In these circumstances, the pri-ority is to lower body temperature. Remove all clothing and cover your child with a damp bed-sheet, fanning them continuous-ly. Prompt hospital treatment is essential.

Natural remedies

- Add the juice of a lemon or lime to a small glass of soda water, and sip.

- Small sips of fresh ginger tea, made with root ginger, will help.

- Fresh cucumber juice sipped in small doses will help the body cool down.

- Homeopathic treatment includes aconite for symptoms of shock, gelsemium when there is accompanying trembling, and conium when lying down feels worse.

'When are we gonna get there?'
said Bunny, kicking the back of the
seat. 'I'm tired of going somewhere.

I want to be there. I want to put on
my bathing suit and play on the beach.'

'Me too.' Both throwing themselves
rhythmically against the seat.

'It's too cold. Only polar bears
go swimming now.'

Annie Proulx
The Shipping News

Travelling companions

Parent's favourites

❀ Any large, snap-together plastic construction bricks, such as stickle bricks, Duplo or Mega Bloks. Losing one or two won't be a great tragedy.

❀ Hand puppets for their outstanding versatility. They are always a mood lifter.

❀ Non-stain, washable colouring pens. Enough said.

❀ A disposable, automatic camera for a kid's eye view of the trip. (Boots make a Photo Bug throw-away. Fisher Price make a kid's first 35mm).

❀ The classic travel toys, Etch a Sketch and Magna Doodle. Pocket versions are now available too.

Toys best avoided

▲ Irreplaceable favourites which might get left behind.

▲ Toys with a seriously heavy battery consumption.

▲ Wax crayons. They melt in the heat.

▲ Play dough which smears, squelches, stains, then tends to dry up and crack.

▲ Talking toys with a mind-numbingly repetitive tone and limited vocabulary.

▲ Toys with lots of crucial parts which can easily get lost, dropped or jammed in tight spots.

Children's favourites

Barbie and Action Man

The stereotyping of so-called boys' toys and girls' toys may have weakened considerably, but two abiding exceptions look set to last out the politically correct 1990s.

Just about every five-year-old girl's favourite, dumb blonde Barbie has an enviable wardrobe and matching accessories. And, in keeping with her latest Generation Girl image, she has rather less time these days for boyfriend Ken and likes to be seen with sister Skipper, baby sister Shelly and best friend Christie. It is no coincidence that they have just as many flashy clothes to collect. Despite her dubious roles as Happenin' Hair, Fruit Fantasy and Bubble Fairy Barbie, you cannot help but admire her staying power.

Another enduring figure, Action Man has tried to cast off his macho image of late. The cropped hair and scar might remain but Action Man's latest personas include Underwater Mission, Arctic Diver, Airport Police, Alpine Sport and Surf Rescue. Some parents may remain disappointed his makers feel obliged to equip him with an automatic pistol and combat knife as readily as a stethoscope and first-aid kit. Find out more at www.actionman.com.

Virtual Pets

Tamagotchis, micro pets, cyberpets – call them what you will – need to be continually fed, petted, put to bed and cleaned up after. It is little wonder some schools had to ban them outright. Still it is testament to the fact that these must-have, hi-tech fads are

Kids have their say

A selection of children were asked what they would take on holiday with them. These are their responses.

- I need my teddy because he loves me. Rose Vicky – aged 2

- I'm going to get my Batman because he likes going on holiday on the train and on the aeroplane. Maverick – aged 3

- I'll bring my Barbies and put some clothes on them. Rosy – aged 3

- I take My Little Pony, because I just do. Claudia – aged 4

- I'm going to bring a big lion. He's called Lion King. He plays with dinosaur, but he doesn't like Big Dolly because he's scared of dollies. Hugo – aged 4

- I like my puppy dog and my penguin best because the puppy is so furry like a pillow, and because the penguin is so little and tiny. Mazy – aged 4

- My Metal Cheetah transformer's great because you can turn it into a human or an aeroplane, and then back to a Metal Cheetah. Samuel – aged 7

- I always take my Furby and a few magazines and, last but not least, a few cuddly things. My Furby's my favourite because it is so sweet and you have to look after it or it will die, and it comes from America to help train you to be a mum. Adrianna – aged 8

guaranteed to keep your kids engrossed. If you are concerned about just how temporary their appeal is likely to be, don't splash out a lot of money. They start from as little as £5/$8. More expensive, but more appealing, is last year's best seller, the interactive Furby, which demands just as much attention, but is, at least, cuddly and cute.

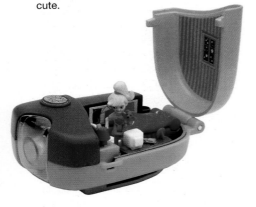

Polly Pocket

The original Bluebird Polly Pocket is being ousted by a Mattel rival. Though the new version is slightly larger and more manageable, it is actually the very titchiness of these cute colourful little worlds that children love. Kids can get lost in the miniature world of make-believe for ages. Yet it is the same petite proportions that can drive parents up the wall. Conducting a fingertip search of the car for a 2cm high Fairy Princess is unlikely to fit into your travel plans. Before the tiny inhabitants have a chance to disappear, be sure to place the toy on a small tray, or into the centre of a lipped plate or bowl and insist that the toy stays put.

Pokémon frenzy

Already massive in Japan and the USA is Nintendo's latest interactive game, Pokémon (an abbreviation of Pocket Monsters). The object of the game is to collect all 150 Pokémon. Each one has a character and ability all of its own. Once captured and tamed, they can be swapped around with friends eager to be first to reach the ultimate status of Pokémon Master.

Pokémon is already such a phenomenon that in America a black market has emerged in its spin-off trading cards with packs selling at four times their street value. There are already 11,000 web sites dedicated to Pokémon. Be warned though. Pokémon is bound for British shores this autumn and it is going to be huge. Find out more on the Nintendo Hotline © UK (023) 8065 2222.

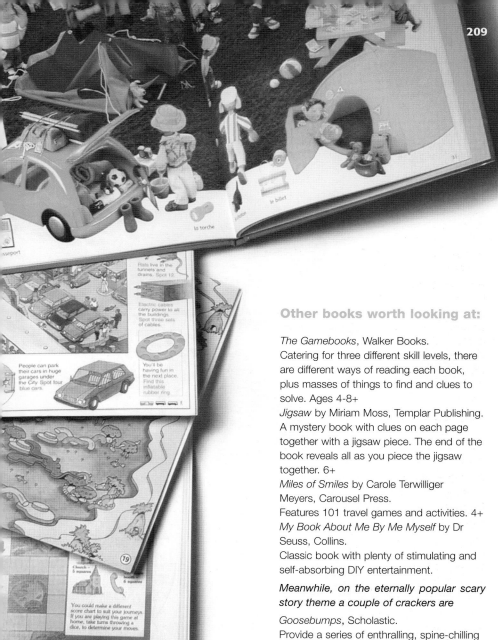

Other books worth looking at:

The Gamebooks, Walker Books.
Catering for three different skill levels, there are different ways of reading each book, plus masses of things to find and clues to solve. Ages 4-8+

Jigsaw by Miriam Moss, Templar Publishing. A mystery book with clues on each page together with a jigsaw piece. The end of the book reveals all as you piece the jigsaw together. 6+

Miles of Smiles by Carole Terwilliger Meyers, Carousel Press.
Features 101 travel games and activities. 4+

My Book About Me By Me Myself by Dr Seuss, Collins.
Classic book with plenty of stimulating and self-absorbing DIY entertainment.

Meanwhile, on the eternally popular scary story theme a couple of crackers are

Goosebumps, Scholastic.
Provide a series of enthralling, spine-chilling tales.

The Weird World by Anthony Masters, Bloomsbury. Fast-paced and quirky, but not overly gross. 8+

preparing your child

Some children are natural travellers and take to new places with the minimum of fuss, often finding it easier than their parents to adapt. Others find going away to be a frightening experience because the new environment is too different or too much to take in. Sometimes children don't want to go away at all – to a child or teenager a friend's birthday party can seem more of a draw than three weeks by a palm-lined beach. Whatever the case, preparing your children makes a big difference to how easily they adapt.

This section aims to help you deal with some of the sticky social situations you are sure to face once you decide to travel overseas with your brood, and to answer some common worries that children have about going away.

But all my friends are here!

Leaving family and friends behind at home, does not have to interfere with your children's' social life. In fact it is easy for your kids' social life to become even more buoyant when they travel overseas.

Why can't my friends come too?

Separated from their cosy circle of friends, travelling away from home can actually be an enriching learning experience for children. From the start nurseries, then later schools, streamline them towards an accepted peer group. Before long they get used to mixing with a limited crowd. Yet holiday time rarely guarantees a convenient group of playmates of the same age and gender, and that is no bad thing. The more you get to utilize this valuable social potential, the more your children will benefit in the long run. You will soon find that the more kids travel, the less they are concerned about who they play with, and the more versatile they become at mixing with all types of new people.

Don't want to!

Naturally, children new to travel may need some reassurance to overcome their shyness at approaching strangers. Do not be surprised if even your normally outgoing and assertive three-year-old suddenly becomes coy and clingy. Encourage your children and help them to make new playmates, but do not insist on it. Talk about different ways to join in or start up a game and think together of different ways to strike up a conversation.

- Hi, I'm Rosey. What's your name?
- Where do you live?
- Do you like football? How about drawing?
- Have you got any brothers or sisters?
- Do you want to see my toys?

Rest assured, the more you travel, and the longer your family trips, the more your children will gain in confidence.

Aren't you coming too, Mum?

Of course, one added bonus of getting kids together is the opportunities it presents for parents to meet up and share a few words. As we grow older, chance meetings become far less frequent. Children provide a common bond. Parents are always eager to strike up a friendly conversation and exchange stories. And seeing you in action only can only serve to boost your children's own social relationships.

But I don't know what they are saying!

Children don't always need words. Once they are immersed in play they are often completely oblivious to who says what, or even who understands, so long as they are all able to get on and have a good time. Yet without the benefit of a common language you may find that, the older your children become, the more intimidating they will find it to approach other kids. Sharing just a few words of the local language can really help break the ice. Music and song are always invaluable communication tools and can help to bridge linguistic and cultural chasms. If any of your children play a musical instrument, consider taking it along with you. Over time, of course, your children will come to realize that attitude is far more important to communication than language.

So where are all the other kids?

If you find yourself staying at accommodation where there are other families, you are unlikely to have any difficulty finding playmates for your kids. Family resorts, hotels and cruise ships are especially good options. Their supervised children's clubs and programmes just about guarantee the company of other children.

The beach is always a good place to meet other children too. This is one place where kids could not care less about communicating properly. Splashing about in the water, building sandcastles and playing volleyball require few words, just plenty of energy and enthusiasm: something children do not have a problem delivering.

If you are on your own, plonk your towels and beach goodies down near to a family you like the look of and let the kids gradually move closer to one another. Curiosity won't let them keep apart for long. The more versatile and innovative toys you bring along, the more likely you are to draw an interested audience. You will normally find other kids tend to hang around, watching from a distance. It is always a good sign they are keen to get involved. Given some time, and a little encouragement, they won't be able to resist joining in.

I don't fit in!

While you are busy acclimatizing yourself, try to imagine what it is like to be your kids in a new environment full of strangers. Be aware of the impact that fitting in can have on your children. It is important to them to be popular and, if one of them seems to be finding it difficult to make friends, try to spot anything that may be making them vulnerable to being picked on or ignored. Do not try to fix it yourself, but encourage some suggestions to boost their self-belief. Is it their clothes, their attitude, their behaviour or what?

Transient friendships are often much less forgiving, and being rebuffed can really shake a kid's confidence. The last thing you want is them feeling desperate to belong. This can create a fragile situation. Trying too hard may leave your child obliged to behave in all the wrong ways just to impress the crowd. Remember, the bigger a ready-made group of friends, the less likely they are to tolerate outsiders. If your kids

As a single child, George is always on the lookout for other kids. He regards children of all ages as potential playmates and is perfectly happy to approach them, wherever we happen to be. A close-knit group may reject him, yet he often perseveres unabashed and nearly always wins them over. I am mightily impressed (and a little envious) of his independence and lack of inhibitions. Yet he is still only three. I can only put this social versatility down to his already diverse travel experiences.

the author

are still new to the game, get them to concentrate on just one or two children at a time instead.

How about the city?

In cosmopolitan places where children are used to hearing different accents and languages, such as the cities of Europe, children tend to be far less affected by language differences and much more relaxed towards foreigners. This makes them easier to meet.

If you are heading for a city, look into organized activities for your children before you leave home. The local tourist office should be able to provide you with a schedule of sports courses and summer camps. Seek out any local newspapers and newsletters too, especially those that target families. These are likely to list activity clubs and organizations, and many may offer children's day camps during the school holidays. Ask at a local newsagents, library or town hall for details. Nearby schools and playgroups listed in the Yellow Pages (or its local equivalent) are usually friendly enough to approach for advice. If all else fails, head straight for the playground at the local park, where you are sure to find other families willing to give you some pointers.

You can trust me!

Once your children become teenagers, there is a good chance they will start to think about only one thing most of the time:

the opposite sex. Once you have discussed your obvious concerns, give them some freedom to explore. So long as they know where they can reach you and what time you are expecting them back, trust in their common sense and let them call some of the shots.

But I don't want to go home yet!

If someone special comes along, try to allow your kids extra time with their newfound friends. When it is time to leave, do not be surprised if there are a few tears or worse. It may help to talk about how friendships come and go, that some last a lifetime and others a day, and that they are all equally important. Consider taking a few snaps of your children playing together. These can be immensely valuable mementos, especially in developing countries where only the wealthiest families are likely to be able to afford a camera. If you take photographs of your children with other kids they meet, be sure to jot down the other family's address and get your child to send copies of the photographs. The time and expense are minimal, especially when you consider that these may be the only photos the other family will ever own of themselves or their children.

If your children make new friends and find it too hard to say goodbye, see that they set up a pen-pal arrangement. These kind of exchanges can last for years and can add a lot of credo back at school.

Index